Critical Acclaim for
The Canadian Small Business Survival Guide

"If anyone is running a small business, or in fact wants to find out about running a business in a theoretical sense, it's a must buy ... full of tremendous information."

Michel Trottier
CBC Radio

"... a wealth of information about a variety of topics ... well written and easy to understand."

Canadian Banker

"... like attending a condensed summer course on small business ... looks at advanced subject matter such as taxation, marketing, inventory control, financing, balance sheet analysis and case studies ..."

Financial Post

"Another strength is the book's Canadian content; information on government programs, tax law, and financing "zeros" in on precisely what the Canadian entrepreneur needs to know."

Canadian Small Business Magazine
(Profit)

D1225384

THE CANADIAN SMALL BUSINESS SURVIVAL GUIDE

How to Start and Operate Your Own
Successful Business

REVISED AND EXPANDED EDITION

Benj Gallander, MBA

THE DUNDURN GROUP
TORONTO · OXFORD

Publisher: Anthony Hawke
Designer: Jennifer Scott
Printer: AGMV Marquis

National Library of Canada Cataloguing in Publication Data

Gallander, Benjamin, 1957–

The Canadian small business survival guide: how to
    start and operate your own successful business

Includes bibliographical references and index.
ISBN 1-55002-377-2

1. New business enterprises — Canada. 2. Small business — Canada.
3. Self-employment — Canada. I. Title.

HD62.7.G35 2002   658.1'141   C2002-901075-6

1 2 3 4 5   06 05 04 03 02

THE CANADA COUNCIL | LE CONSEIL DES ARTS
FOR THE ARTS | DU CANADA
SINCE 1957 | DEPUIS 1957

Canada

ONTARIO ARTS COUNCIL
CONSEIL DES ARTS DE L'ONTARIO

We acknowledge the support of the **Canada Council for the Arts** and the **Ontario Arts Council** for our publishing program. We also acknowledge the financial support of the **Government of Canada** through the **Book Publishing Industry Development Program** and **The Association for the Export of Canadian Books,** and the **Government of Ontario** through the **Ontario Book Publishers Tax Credit** program.

Care has been taken to trace the ownership of copyright material used in this book. The author and the publisher welcome any information enabling them to rectify any references or credit in subsequent editions.

J. Kirk Howard, President

Printed and bound in Canada.⊛
Printed on recycled paper.
www.dundurn.com

Dundurn Press	Dundurn Press	Dundurn Press
8 Market Street	73 Lime Walk	2250 Military Road
Suite 200	Headington, Oxford,	Tonawanda NY
Toronto, Ontario, Canada	England	U.S.A. 14150
M5E 1M6	OX3 7AD	

THE CANADIAN
SMALL BUSINESS
SURVIVAL GUIDE

Contents

CHARTS, CHECKLISTS, EXHIBITS, GRAPHS, AND TABLES

ACKNOWLEGEMENTS

A number of people have been wonderful in helping me put this book together, and to them I express my deep appreciation for their aid and their friendship. Some of these people include:

Carol Pauker, who has spent many hours turning my "English" into a real, comprehensive language. Carol's knack of criticizing constructively and initiating improvements is an art;

David Ossea, who also has spent numerous hours editing this work. I would be remiss if I did not mention that David turns a great pivot on the double play;

Ben Stadelmann, who contributed the case "Barb's Blues" and is my business partner at *Contra the Heard* Investment Letter;

Max Abramowitz, who contributed the chapter on Computers for Small Business and the Internet for Small Business and is my guide when in New York;

Ellen Pauker, Mike Speyer, Ellissa Gallander, Tony Hawke, Nancy Turk, Todd Vercoe, and Candy Pauker, who have lent their skills in various aspects of this guide.

Thanks.

Preface to the First Edition

The intended audience for this guide is any individual who is interested in starting, or has recently started, a business in Canada. It is designed to satisfy the needs of people whose business knowledge is limited, and also those people who are prepared to move on to more sophisticated operational techniques.

Approximately 50 percent of businesses fail within two years of start-up. Within five years, over 80 percent of the ventures no longer exist. One of the reasons for this dismal performance, I feel, has been the lack of a good book on how to start and operate a business in Canada. I became acutely aware of this void in the book market when I began teaching at the college level. Though I used the best text I could, find, neither my students nor I were satisfied with it.

For this reason, I decided to write the definitive Canadian book on starting and operating a successful small business, and I believe I have succeeded. To do this, I relied on my experiences in personal business, consulting, teaching, and writing. By blending these areas, I have written an easy-to-read, easy-to-understand, small business guide.

The guide consists of text, exhibits, checklists, and cases covering all facets of starting a business. It is designed so that the reader has the option, not only to read the book, but to participate. Through various exercises, many real life business situations are experienced; options are pondered before the problems are solved.

This book also includes a numerical section. I have structured this part to be accessible even to those with limited mathematical experience. It is vital to have a good grasp of the numbers behind business. Some books neglect this numerical section, but that is akin to teaching someone to build a house without a strong foundation. The structure may stand for a short time, but collapse is inevitable.

This guide is designed to help the reader decide first, if a business venture is worthwhile; and, second, to provide the materials to help it thrive. If properly used, I believe the book will be an invaluable tool for the entrepreneur.

Preface to the Second Edition

The purpose of the second edition is to update and revise the first edition. As the world of business is ever changing, it is important that a book of this sort evolves with the times. Since the first printing of *The Canadian Small Business Survival Guide* three years ago, I have kept closely abreast of any changes that should be incorporated into this second edition. At the same time, an eye has been kept towards the future so that this edition will remain current.

One of the major recent government initiative has been the implementation of the GST and an appendix has been added to cover this. Care has been taken to explain this area as simply as possible so that some of the recent confusion concerning this topic might be overcome. Requests have also been made to add information on a "Partnership Agreement" and this has been done through the addition of a checklist in another appendix. Also, numerous addresses have changed in the past few years and these have been updated.

Operating a small business is not a simple task and that will not change. Take the time necessary to read this book and then carefully assess whether or not you have the ingredients to start your own enterprise. For those of you who choose to start, this can be one the most rewarding "adventures" of your life. I wish you the best in your venture.

Preface to the Third Edition

It has been over a decade since *The Canadian Small Business Survival Guide* hit the bookstores. A bestseller for years, this third edition happens to coincide with its tenth printing. Few Canadian books have remained in constant demand for almost thirteen years. Adoptions of the work have been written for China, the Czech Republic, and the United States. In addition, specific sections of the book sold in over a dozen countries.

The world today is in many significant respects a far different place than it was in 1988. I remember writing the manuscript on a typewriter, and then retyping it all again with the edits. How antiquated that seems in a world with computer word processors today! Then, the word Internet was unknown to the common lexicon, and e-commerce just an avant-garde concept.

These technological advances have made globalization a reality, something few could fathom in that recently bygone era. Many major corporations are now mega-corporations, with offices and retail outlets extending throughout the globe. In some respects, walking down the Champs-Elysees in Paris is not much different from ambling down Fifth Avenue in New York. The distinctiveness of various cultures has eroded under the "New World Order."

Yet, even in the highly competitive commercial terrain of the New World, there remains a niche for the small business. In fact, small enterprises with the smarts are thriving, and in many cases better serving their markets than the big corporations. Naturally, amidst the array of successes, there are failures, as starting a successful small business remains difficult to do.

This third edition is different in some ways from its predecessors. A chapter on the Internet was added and the computerization chapter has been significantly overhauled. Addresses to resources for entrepreneurs have been updated, and several other enhancements have been included.

If you have questions, comments, or suggestions on how to improve this book, I would be happy to hear from you. In the meantime, I wish you the best of luck with your business!

Benj Gallander
www.contratheheard.com
Email: gall@pathcom.com

To My Parents

PART I

What is a "Small" Business?

It is fairly easy to walk down the street and identify the various "mom and pop" shops as small businesses. But what is it that small businesses have in common, that separates them from medium and large organizations? By identifying a number of characteristics, not all of which apply to every small business, we can gain insight into this type of venture.

A) Independently Owned and Operated

Almost all small businesses are independently owned and operated, usually by the same person(s). This fact leaves the responsibility and decision-making process to the owner(s). Like most rules, this requires some qualifications, especially when one thinks of franchises. For, as demonstrated later in the book, franchisees are indeed operating their own business, but without the independence that characterizes most small business operators.

B) Not Dominant in the Field

Small businesses do not dominate in their field and, therefore, have an extremely limited share of the overall marketplace. Generally, firms with larger sales volumes, more employees, and greater resources within the industry often force the smaller ventures to find and serve a "market niche" (a specialized area of the marketplace) based on their location and/or their product or service. Larger firms do not find it worthwhile to serve this marketplace.

C) Area of Operations is Local

Small businesses may have markets in diverse locations, but their operations are based in one area. The majority of owners and workers live near this site.

D) Capital and Ownership is Provided by One Person or a Small Group

Usually, the larger the pool of capital available to the new venture, the greater the ultimate business size; therefore, characteristically, small businesses have capital supplied by one person or a small number of parties.

E) Government Parameters

By analyzing certain government directives, small businesses can be quantified. Numerous federal and provincial government programmes base their qualifications for small business on sales levels up to $2,000,000, and profit levels no greater than $200,000. These restrictions apply to the availability of tax benefits, hiring programmes, and many government grants and subsidies. These programmes are discussed later in the book.

F) Employee Categorizations

A particularly useful indicator to the size of a business is its number of employees. A manufacturing firm with fewer than 100 employees is generally considered to be a small business, while other business sectors are limited to 50 workers. Many experts choose this category as one of the most important when considering business size, because the number of employees remains unaffected by inflation.

Because a manufacturing firm usually needs a much larger number of employees, this type of organization with sales of five to ten million dollars is often considered to be small. A service or retail organization, with this level of sales, would be classified as a medium-sized operation.

TYPES OF SMALL BUSINESSES

There are four major types of small businesses: manufacturing, service, wholesale, and retail. Each of these businesses has its own characteristics and risks.

The Manufacturing Business

Manufacturing is the conversion of raw materials into a useful product; there are two types of manufacturing to consider: primary and secondary. Primary is the processing of basic new materials, such as uranium, silver, or petroleum. These can be used in a further process called secondary manufacturing, which is the production of finished goods that can be sold to a wholesaler, retailer, or perhaps directly to the consumer.

Beginning a manufacturing firm requires a tremendous amount of capital; therefore, it is most suitable for a large business with more resources; however, despite the risks, small manufacturers do exist. This is because manufacturing can create a tremendous financial return, often above 20 percent. Foreseeably, many small firms end up by the wayside due to their lack of capital and/or knowledge.

It is worthwhile noting that many great innovators began as small manufacturers, using their ingenuity to compete with the larger firms, which have many competitive advantages.

The Service Business

Services sell personal skills rather than products to their clientele. Typical examples of services include: the barber, daycare centres, television repair shops, and consultants. In the past decade, the service sector has led the growth for small businesses. This is largely because services require a limited amount of capital investment; fulfil the desires of individuals who are growing richer with the economy; and can be operated from the home. Recently, there has been a trend to franchise service businesses. This has proven to be extremely successful as individuals license their "recipe" for prosperity.

The Wholesale Business

Wholesalers are in the middle between manufacturers and retailers. Essentially, they buy products from the manufacturers, store them, and then resell to retailers, or more rarely, to the consumer.

As middle people, a substantial portion of the wholesaler's time is spent working as a diplomat, ensuring that suppliers provide goods on time, and soothing retailers when goods arrive late. It is important that the wholesaler is skilful at this task, as customers tend to be fewer and larger; therefore, each customer represents a substantial portion of the middle person's business, and poor diplomacy can cause an appreciable decline in sales.

Small businesses do the major portion of the wholesaling business in Canada.

The Retail Business

Retailers buy products from manufacturers, wholesalers, jobbers, or other distributors, and sell them to the consumer. Small business dominates this area; the majority of operators have fewer than five employees.

There are hundreds of kinds of retailers from small grocery stores to variety stores to specialty shops. One of the key success variables for these firms is a convenient location, as customers are often not willing to travel far for their purchase.

The characteristics of the different business types: manufacturing, service, wholesale, and retail do vary, as do the risks associated with each of these sectors. But most of the rules and methods for starting and operating a successful small business apply to all of these types. Variables in rules and methods, as they apply to a sector, will be indicated in the book.

CAN SMALL BUSINESSES COMPETE?

Large business versus small business has become an increasingly important issue as more organizations are growing larger and larger, choosing to take advantage of the factors that give size a competitive edge. Large enterprises do have many advantages over the smaller firm.

One of the major advantages is "economies of scale." Economies of scale means that the larger the organization, the lower the cost per unit to reach the marketplace. This occurs because the increased size produces increased efficiencies, creating economies for lowering costs. An example is the larger firm that can buy in quantity and, therefore, obtain discounts from suppliers. This is an advantage that will lower "per unit" costs and is unavailable to the small firm. Another example of an economy of scale is the larger firm that can distribute in volume, therefore, their per unit distribution cost will be less than it would be for the smaller enterprise.

Major corporations can also take advantage of advertising economies. Because of their large promotional budgets, a greater selection of media types are available in which to advertise, and often the time or space can be purchased at a reduced cost. This allows the large enterprise to reach its potential consumers at a lower cost per person.

Larger enterprises also have other competitive advantages. They can carry more products or deliver more services than the "little guy." This fact will appeal to the consumer who wants greater selection or prefers "one-stop" shopping.

Some customers also desire to deal exclusively with larger enterprises, convinced that the quality of the product might be higher, or more confident in the guarantee if the product proves defective.

Also, when the economy is experiencing difficulties, larger firms have the resources to "tough out" the times, while the economic downturn can quickly bankrupt the small business.

Other advantages often sited for large firms include tax advantages, government incentives, and the ability to hire better employees. These reasons though rarely apply, as small businesses have opportunities in these areas.

Though larger businesses do have many advantages, small businesses are thriving across the nation due to their own set of competitive advantages. One major advantage small businesses often experience is greater loyalty from both customers and employees. Many customers enjoy dealing with the small business, primarily because of the service they receive. In addition to this, knowing that the owner is nearby and can quickly remedy a situation is comforting. Employees also prefer dealing with the boss rather than with a faceless corporate head. If the employee has a suggestion or problem, the option to walk right up to the owner and state his case exists. This gives the employee additional input into how his actions might affect the business and work situation.

Another example favourable to the small business is flexibility. When products or services change, or the market undergoes a transformation, the small operation can often respond more quickly than the giant. Instead of having to struggle through the ranks of bureaucratic decision-making, an owner can quickly change tack. Coupled with this is the fact that small firms can usually innovate quickly if there is a market opportunity. Though large organizations will have greater resources to change, the small enterprise can capitalize on the presence of a specific market niche that might develop or need servicing.

Small businesses also have a competitive advantage when fast service in a local market is of the essence. This if often the case with perishable goods, where products must reach the consumer quickly. In this instance, it is usually not beneficial for a larger operation to enter the marketplace.

In industry in recent years, the trend had been towards "bigger is better." But small businesses maintain competitive advantages that are allowing them to thrive within the marketplace. In the business domain, there is sufficient room for various sized firms, satisfying the diverse needs of the marketplace.

WHY BUSINESSES FAIL
(to be read when you are in the mood to become depressed)

There are countless reasons why businesses fail, a number of which will be discussed in this section. By understanding the major reasons for failure, many of these pitfalls can be avoided. As mentioned previously, approximately eighty percent of the firms that commence operations do not exist after five years. This indicates various kinds of mismanagement, and many individuals who should not attempt to begin their enterprises.

A) Inexperience
Experience is a key ingredient for operating a successful business. Without it the operation is almost guaranteed to fail. Entering a field without experience is ideal for a masochist with time and money to blow.

B) Inadequate Capital
Many novice entrepreneurs attempt to commence their businesses without sufficient funding. Since they are uneducated in calculating the dollars necessary to begin their ventures, they underestimate costs, and encounter a shortfall before they can possibly make a sale. More common though, is the individual who opens the business, but does not recognize the costs associated with the day-to-day operations, and therefore, does not plan for this period. As the vast majority of ventures lose money for the first year, and often for the second, funds must be available to operate during this time. Cash flow forecasting can help to plan for this. (See "Cash Flow" section.)

C) Inadequate Sales
Inadequate sales may be the result of a number of factors. Perhaps the business simply does not have an item consumers want. Maybe

the marketing strategy is poor, or the location does not have the necessary traffic flow. Regardless of the root cause, a firm cannot survive without adequate sales. The best method of knowing if a market exists for your product is experience.

D) High Operating Costs

Expenses in a new operation must be carefully controlled. Often, the neophyte entrepreneur becomes enveloped in grandiose plans or simply does not have the knowledge to control costs, with the result that expenses skyrocket and bills cannot be paid. This will lead to quick financial ruin. A new operation must often cut corners, reducing costs wherever reasonable. This does not mean that a shoddy product or service should be presented to the public. It does mean that the entrepreneur should focus on the key elements that will produce sales, and reduce those expenses that will not have a "real" effect on the revenue level. Remember: a new business usually has limited financial resources and, therefore, efforts must be made to utilize the resources wisely.

E) Inability to Compete

Sometimes a business cannot compete because of limited expertise, limited buying power, or other factors. Entrepreneurs who find themselves in this situation can either fold up shop, or attempt to think of a new method to market the business.

F) Poor Location

Poor location selection can easily lead to a business failure, therefore, an entrepreneur should take time when choosing the site for the venture.

G) Lack of Formulation of Plan or Goals

Many people commence their operation without a clear-cut direction. This lack of planning often can result in bankruptcy. The formation of a business plan forces the entrepreneur to focus on goals and objectives, and set in place a time frame in which to meet them. (See "The Business Plan" section.)

H) Lack of Self-Evaluation

Many people are infatuated with the idea of running their own enterprise. Unfortunately, they lack the characteristics necessary to be a successful entrepreneur. They might lack drive or ambition or discipline for instance. (See the next section on "You".)

I) Cash Flow

Inadequate cash flow can easily "strangle" a fledging operation. The venture must have an adequate capital inflow to meet its obligations. Many entrepreneurs do not plan for the times when they will have a cash flow shortage (See "Cash Flow" section).

J) Money Taken Out of Business

Many entrepreneurs are greedy. As money flows into the business, they take funds out of the business. This can leave the enterprise with a shortage of operating funds. In almost every case, money earned by the venture in its first few years of operation should be reinvested in the enterprise.

K) Poor Bookkeeping

When the bookkeeping is poor, it is difficult to know the financial situation of the business. This can lead to decisions that are not in accordance with the financial position of the venture (See "Bookkeeping").

L) Accounts Receivable Too High

Accounts receivable *must* be collected, and the quicker they are, the better for the bottom line. In this one area being too nice can work against you. A plan to collect these receivables is a major tool (See "Collect Those Accounts Receivable!" section).

M) Inventory Too High

Inventory mismanagement was one the major problems that plagued businesses in the last recession. While it is important to avoid being out of stock and to take quantity discounts when buying, it is also of great importance not to have inventory sit on the shelves too long. This is a waste of money. Inventory control saves money and generates income.

N) Too Much Capital Into Fixed Assets

The major decisions that the entrepreneur must make when considering purchasing an asset are twofold. First, whether it is really needed. Second, whether it should be bought or leased. The decisions must be made with the total resources of the enterprise in mind, in order to ensure that sufficient funds for working capital and other purposes remain.

O) Lousy Employees

You have probably been in a situation in which an employee is rude, and makes you feel as though your patronage is not desired at his workplace. Employees like this can be very costly for a business. In addition to this, dishonest workers can cause an enterprise to fail.

P) Other Reasons for Failure

Some of the other reasons that businesses fail include the owner's ill health; disagreements among partners; fraud; marital difficulties; improper insurance; and changing economic conditions.

By focusing on these reasons before you enter a business, you might decide that starting an enterprise is not for you. This is not necessarily a failure, but might be a logical way to save time, energy, and money.

If you do choose to start a business, or have already commenced refer to the "Reasons Businesses Fail" now and again. By doing this, you might recognize one of these situations and take the necessary steps to avoid insolvency.

THE PROS AND CONS OF OPERATING YOUR OWN BUSINESS

Before you commence your enterprise, it is extremely important that you evaluate both the rewards you earn and the risks you will encounter. Many individuals choose to "jump right in" without carefully analyzing the effect that the business will have on their lives. An examination of the pros and cons of self-employment might discourage you from beginning your own venture, but it is better to decide that self-employment is not for you before you invest substantial amounts of time, money, and energy; rather than later, when you realize that you have made one of the biggest mistakes of your life.

The Pros of Operating Your Own Business

A) You Can Be Your Own Boss

Many people are tired of working for someone else. They want to experience the independence that is achieved by becoming self-employed. In many surveys, being one's own boss and being independent, rank as the major reasons that people enjoy being in business for themselves.

B) The Profits Are All Yours

Many people feel that they are working largely for the monetary benefit of their employer. When you choose to work for yourself, the profits are retained exclusively by you, and in some cases, by your partners. It is interesting to note that when the pros of operating your own business are analyzed, people often neglect to mention the profit factor. Perhaps the primary reason for this omission is that people do not wish to sound greedy. Profit, in certain respects, has become a dirty word. But yes, it is a vital reason to enjoy self-employment.

C) Additional Creativity

Skills that you are not able to utilize when working for another employer can sometimes be of the utmost importance in making your business a success. Being creative gives a greater sense of achievement, self-confidence, and enjoyment than is experienced when working for someone else.

D) You Can Set Own Hours

To some degree, this is true. But as the cons will indicate, it is certainly not all beer, skittles, and relaxation.

E) You Can Choose Your Employees and Your Customers

Choice can be extremely enjoyable benefit. Instead of working with people you dislike, you can surround yourself with individuals whose company you enjoy; perhaps because their moral values, outlook, and interests are compatible with yours.

F) Tax Advantages

Often, items can be written off that would not be possible if you were working for someone else. Some of these items can include expenses associated with your home or apartment, books, gas, etc. (See Tax section.)

The Cons of Operating Your Own Business

A) The Hours

Yes, you can indeed set your own hours, as was suggested in the pros. But if you only choose to work those hours when the mood strikes, odds are that you will not have an ongoing enterprise, instead a bankrupt business will be in the cards. Generally, entrepreneurs work far more hours than someone who is not self-employed. This is particularly true in the initial stages of operation, when the business must be established and capital must be spent on items besides additional employees. These conditions force you to do work that later, when the business is successful might be delegated. Many novice business people find that the long hours required to establish their business venture are not guarantees of a successful venture, but also can cost them their marriages and family lives. For many, this cost is justifiably too high. It is imperative that when you decide to start a business, you consider those people on whom the decisions will have an impact. Hopefully, their full support will be obtained before you embark on the venture.

B) Lack of Profit and a Regular Pay Cheque

Currently, most of you go to work, and every week or two your pay cheque arrives as regularly as clockwork. Unfortunately, this will not be the case as you establish your own business. As most of you will not be making money for one or two years, you will have to rely on your savings, or perhaps, on family and friends to finance you. Even when the business begins to turn a profit, the tally might be low or irregular. The absence of a Friday pay cheque can make planning your lifestyle more difficult.

C) Failure

As stated previously (and it will be stated again), the odds dictate that you will not be successful with your enterprise. Simply because you are reading this book, your chances of success are increasing, but many will still end up with a failed business. Naturally, failure can be emotionally difficult to cope with, and that may require reliance on tremendous inner strength. In addition to this problem, failure may led to financial ruin. If a positive note can be found here, it is that many of the most successful entrepreneurs are individuals who have failed previously, learned from their mistakes, and managed to avoid the same disasters the second time around. It is to be hoped, though, that you will learn from others' mistakes and make few of your own.

D) Stress

More are more is currently being discovered and written about stress. As the majority of the responsibilities for the business will fall upon your shoulders (and perhaps your partners), stress will be created. For most individuals, stressful situations occur when everything is not happening as designed. This anxiety is too big a burden, and people either crack and become ill from the strain, or they decide that being self-employed is not worth the cost.

Being self-employed has numerous advantages and disadvantages. The pros and cons must be carefully weighed before the decision to start a business is made.

Chart 1-1

Starting and Operating Your Own Business	
Pros	**Cons**
A. You can be your own boss (independence). B. The profits are all yours. C. Additional creativity. D. You can set your own hours. E. You can choose your employ ees and your customers. F. Tax advantages.	A. The hours B. Lack of profits and a regular paycheque. C. Failure D. Stress.

THREE CRITICAL QUESTIONS

What business am I going into?
What are my business goals and objectives?
What are my personal goals and objectives?

What Business am I going into?

As you use this book, the nature of your prospective business will become more and more clear. Some individuals decide that they want to open a bookstore, but they do not think beyond the fact that they enjoy reading and wish to be surrounded by books. Owning a bookstore consists of deciding what market you want to reach, choosing the books for the public, buying the books, stocking the shelves, meeting people every day, predicting future buying trends, and numerous other activities. A complete description of the nature of the venture should be written long before you enter the field.

What are my business goals and objectives?

Perhaps you want to have a multinational corporation. Maybe your dream is to own a small café where friends can drop in and chat. Perhaps you want to have a business that has no employees because you enjoy working by yourself. Maybe a primary concern is to produce the finest quality product. Before commencing operations, carefully analyze your business goals and objectives. This will give you a clearer focus.

What are my personal goals and objectives?

Do you want to be rich? Do you want to relax in the country and fish all day? Do you want to spend lots of time with your family? Whatever your personal goals and objectives might be, make certain that they are compatible with your business goals and objectives. If your business goal is to have a multinational corporation, and your personal goal is to spend more time with your family, the two are incompatible. A change in personal goals and objectives must occur, or another business must be found.

When planning your personal and business goals, think of both the short-term and long-term goals. This will help you to see if the goals are compatible over time.

By answering these three questions and making certain that the answers are compatible a far clearer concept about your potential enterprise will be gleaned. This will serve as a framework for the short-term and long-term enjoyment of your new venture.

FIVE KEY INGREDIENTS FOR BUSINESS SUCCESS

Five crucial needs for a small business are: 1) a good idea for a product or service; 2) knowledge and experience in the business area; 3) sufficient capital to start and operate the business; 4) a battle plan; and 5) a sufficient market.

1) Idea: Product or Service

If you plan to enter a business, there must be something to sell. This is really as basic as it gets. You might feel that you want to start your own business, but not have a clue about what that business will be. Perhaps by analyzing your daily activities, you will arrive at a potential business idea. Maybe the field that you work in would be ideal, or perhaps the business might arise out of an expanded hobby. Perhaps a friend has a wonderful idea and a partnership can be formed. The key is that the concept must be generated from somewhere; otherwise it is impossible to start a business.

2. Knowledge and Experience

Knowledge and experience are both essential to being successful in business. An understanding of the marketplace, suppliers, operations, and the various other facets of the venture can be obtained most thoroughly by working in the field prior to the commencement of the venture. Without this "tutelage," the odds for success of the venture decrease rapidly.

Many people attempt to enter a field in which they have extremely limited experience. The perfect example of this is the budding restaurateur. Yes, he does eat, and yes, he knows just what he likes to see on the menu, but no, that does not mean that he can open and successfully operate a restaurant. Experience means seeing the operation form the inside, knowing the different aspects that make the business tick. Knowledge is critical to success, and I cannot emphasize the experiential aspect of business success strongly enough.

Before you enter commerce spend time in the field that you are contemplating. Ideally, you will gain experience and knowledge over a number of years, as you learn every aspect of the trade, and plan on applying the learning to your own operation. By doing this, you greatly increase the chances of being one of the approximately 50 percent of businesses that exist two years after start-up, and one of the twenty percent of businesses which survive for five years.

Virtually every consultant, teacher, or businessperson will stress the importance of knowledge and experience before starting a venture. Take this advice to heart.

3. Capital

Many businesses fail because they do not have sufficient start-up and operating capital. Quite often, an individual has enough money to begin the venture, but once the enterprise is operational, the business folds because of an insufficient capital base to cover the outflow of funds. You might have the best idea in the world, but without the necessary funding, the idea should never have become more than a business plan.

Unfortunately, to begin virtually every business, capital is necessary. Since most small businesses have limited resources to start, the venture must be planned accordingly. Limited resources necessitates cutting corners; inexpensive carpeting where the Persian rugs "should" be, basic chairs instead of executive seats for all visitors, lunches from home instead of dining at the Ritz. The key is to live within the means of the business. Gradually, with success, you will be able to think about becoming more extravagant. But wait until sufficient profits are being realized.

4. Battle Plan

Many novice entrepreneurs choose to enter commerce with no set direction. A "battle plan" outlining both personal and business goals as well as objectives, and a realistic time frame in which to meet those targets, is essential to the success of a new venture. The battle plan, which will almost always take the format of a business plan, should be as comprehensive as possible. The plan is the complete blueprint from which the business can be operated, setting the targets that you wish to reach, and outlining the methodology with which you hope to reach them.

The creation of the battle plan does require time, energy, and effort. Some entrepreneurs choose to ignore the plan, utilizing a "seat of the pants" technique: coping with each problem as it arises. A small portion of these individuals are even successful. But for the majority of entrepreneurs, the "seat of the pants" technique is a blueprint for failure. Even with clearly defined goals and objectives, success will be difficult to achieve, but without them, success remains unlikely.

5. Market

If you want to be a successful businessperson, you must have people who desire your product or service. Sometimes, you can be in the fortunate position of having pent-up demand, meaning that the market exists and is simply waiting for someone to provide the product or service to fill it. Usually though, you have to make the market realize that your business exists with the product or service the public needs.

The essence of this idea is that a demand must exist for your product or service. Otherwise limited sales, a lack of income, and a venture that cannot survive will be the result.

You!

Ultimately, the key ingredient in making the business a success will be you! To discover if you have the ingredients for entrepreneurship, check yourself candidly against some of these traits. Though it is not critical that you possess all of them, and many successful business people defy the mould that is being cast, research has demonstrated that certain characteristics are usually present for success.

A) Ambition

It is very easy to start a small business. But it is the ambition to succeed in the long-term that will ultimately allow the enterprise to survive and thrive. Many individuals do not have the necessary drive and ambition to continue working at their venture, especially when faced with the difficult problems that almost always occur.

B) Communication Skills

Many individuals have the knowledge to establish an excellent business, but they do not have the communications ability necessary to make the sales to customers, or to motivate employees. Fortunately, if this skill is lacking, in most cases it can be learned.

C) Discipline

Especially in the initial stages of the venture, tremendous discipline will be required to work the long hours necessary. Later, even as the workload lessens slightly, discipline will remain a necessity, especially to tackle the boring, redundant tasks that make distractions so delightful. Often, the most successful owners become workaholics, which presents its own set of problems.

D) Experience and Knowledge

Experience and knowledge — as stated previously — in the field in which you are planning to commence operations are critical for business success. Without these components, failure is almost cer-tifiably guaranteed.

E) Goal Setters

Successful people set realistic goals and work towards them. These goals often become the prime motivations to work day in and day out.

F) Innovative

Innovative skills result in maximum usage of the limited resources of the business. They can turn bad positions into opportunities, good conditions into excellent ones.

G) Leadership Qualities

Most entrepreneurs possess ample leadership abilities. These abilities can be used to motivate employees, complete sales, deal with bankers, earn payment terms from suppliers, just to name a few.

H) Risk-Takers

Successful entrepreneurs are willing to gamble. They do not take excessive, outrageous risks, but reasonable, calculated chances.

I) Self-Confident

Entrepreneurs who succeed are self-confident. They have a strong belief in their ability to survive and thrive. This confi-dence is a tremendous aid when problems appear, as they ulti-mately will.

By assessing yourself against the personal characteristics out-lined, you will have a better idea if you have the necessary ingredi-ents to be an entrepreneur. In some cases, self-assessments are diffi-cult to make. If this is your experience, then ask family and friends whose opinions you value, if they think that you would be a good businessperson. This will help to clarify if you are of the "entrepre-neurial mould."

1. Are you usually a self-starter?
2. When in a group, are you usually one
    of the people who get things going?
3. Do you plan to accomplish certain things
    in a day?
4. Do you feel relaxed when speaking in front
    of your fellow workers?
5. Are you willing to stay up late at night to
    complete an assignment?
6. Would you describe yourself as decisive?
7. Are you able to admit when you have made
    a mistake?
8. Are you willing to tackle areas with which
    you have little familiarity?
9. Do you believe that you control your own
    destiny?
10. Do you get along well with people?
11. Are you willing to take risks even though
    you might fail?
12. Can you say "no" to people when you have
    valid reasons?
13. Do you know what you want to be doing
    in five years?
14. Do you enjoy a challenge?
15. Are you able to keep secrets?
16. Can you bounce back quickly from
    setbacks and failures?

The more questions answered "yes," the better your chance for being a successful entrepreneur.

CASE ANALYSIS

At various points in the book, you will find a case. The purpose of the case is to allow you to utilize the preceding information and to apply it to real-life business situations. This is the technique I used in my courses, and is applied in many business schools.

Essentially, the case describes a situation, and forces you to analyze and formulate an action plan to remedy the difficulties. In certain respects, the cases are not absolutely complete, and, therefore, your decisions must be made by considering elements of uncertainty and risk. This is similar to real-life situations.

The solutions to the cases are towards the end of the book. Sometimes, your decision will vary from the one that I suggest. This does not necessarily make your answer incorrect. The important result is that you carefully analyze the situation, account for the major factors in the case, and develop a solution that is compatible with the key variable in the problem, and with the management's orientation. If, after solving the case, you find that you have missed major difficulties, or your numbers do not match those in the answer section, try the case again until you understand the situation completely. This will help to increase your understanding of starting and operating a business,. By making errors within the content of the guide, instead of when you commence the operation, a great deal of time, money, and effort ultimately will be saved.

The case solution involves five steps: 1) Problem Identification; 2) Sub-Problem Identification; 3) Situation Analysis; 4) Formulating Alternatives; 5) Recommendations.

Problem Identification

In this section, you should highlight one or two of the major problems. These issues will be the most critical difficulties that must be addressed.

Sub-Problem Identification

Here you will identify the less important difficulties presented in the case. These should be ranked in order of priority, as this will ensure that the more important elements will be solved first.

Situation Analysis

In this section, you should arrive at a clear understanding of how the problems occurred. Often, by starting at the first recognizable problem, it becomes easier to see how the whole situation developed, and this can aid in the formulation of a solution. The business should also be analysed, taking into account the business history, the current state of affairs, and how the owner desires the business to evolve. Major environmental issues, such as competition, government regulations, or changes in the marketplace, should also be highlighted if applicable. This has a further bearing on the problems and their solutions.

Formulating Alternatives

Now you are at the point at which you can develop potential solutions for problems and sub-problems. State the most realistic alternatives, highlighting the advantages and disadvantages of each, while establishing a time frame that would be appropriate for the alternatives' implementation. Check to make certain that the alternatives are indeed feasible, given the resources of the business. Focus on the consequences of each decision, and the impact that they will have on the business.

Recommendations

From the alternatives, select the solution(s) that you would choose to implement. Present a plan describing the implementation process, explaining how the solution(s) would achieve the desired goals of the enterprise, and how, once the plan is implemented, you would evaluate the results.

Certainly, you are gaining valuable knowledge and insight by reading about starting and operating a business, but further knowledge will be added by preparing, analyzing, and formulating solutions to the cases. By doing this, you can gain a certain experiential level of business operations that is certainly not as complete as commencing the venture, but is more practical than merely reading about starting the operation.

CASE 1: THE DECISION

Jon Sanders was having a difficult time making a decision. He had been working for a major retail department store for thirteen years, the last five as store manager.

"You know, Bette," he began to his wife who was six months pregnant with their third child, "I really want to start that outdoor store. We've got a city with a population of 50,000 people and not one specialty store for the outdoor enthusiast. It's an untapped market."

"I've supported you on this idea for years, Jon. If you want to start the store, I'm behind you," Bette responded.

Jon Sanders had an excellent employment record. When he began at the department store, he worked in the "Sporting and Outdoor Life" section, an assignment that he enjoyed immensely, as he was always a self-described "sports and camping nut." After four years in this department, he was elevated to floor manager; four years after he became the store manager. Store sales, since Jon had taken over, increased by 92 percent, the third largest increase in the 54-store chain. Many people attributed this success to the fact that Jon was hardworking and diligent, got along well with those he supervised, and had an intuitive sense for what would sell in the local market.

Lately though, Jon had been restless at work. He enjoyed the job, but found that the challenge was waning. There were rumours of a promotion to the head office in Vancouver, but Jon was not excited about the prospect of moving.

Though Jon had not done any market research, he was certain that a specialized outdoor store would do a tremendous amount of business, as the city was filled with avid campers, hikers, and fisherman. There were a couple of appropriate locations near downtown that Jon had inquired about, and both of the landlords—who knew Jon well from shopping at the department store—said that they would be happy to have him as a tenant.

Bette had worked as a legal secretary until the birth of their first child, four years ago. She loved spending time with the children, but was anxious to return to work. The couple had agreed that after the birth of their third and last planned child, Bette would return to a job.

Jon and Bette had purchased a house before Tyler, the second child, was born. The house had cost $165,000 of which $75,000 was still owed on the mortgage. Jon and Bette planned to do renovations in a couple of years so that each of the children would have their own bedroom. This would not be the case when the baby was born in a few months time.

What should Jon do?

PART II

CYCLES

Before staring your business, it is important to consider the cycles that will have an impact on your venture. Seasonal cycles, the business cycle, and the product life cycle should all be considered.

Seasonal Cycles

For some businesses, especially those that produce necessities such as bread, seasonal cycles do not exist, as people purchase this item regularly throughout the year. On the other hand, the demand for skiing in this country will vary greatly, determined by a number of factors. The first factor is the season. The vast majority of skiing occurs in the winter months, with some autumn and spring skiing in certain areas of the country. For those involved in the skiing industry then, these seasonal variations for sales must be planned for, as revenues outside of the winter months will be negligble or non-existent; therefore, owners of ski resorts, those who manufacture ski equipment, and hotels and caterers who are dependent on the industry, must prepare their operations so that they have sufficient cash on hand to survive the lean months.

For many retailers the Christmas months of November and December comprise about 50 percent of their annual sales volume. To prepare for this, consideration must be given to short-term financing to buy inventory in the fall; seasonal employee hirings; when to promote the business; and numerous other factors. Adjusting your operation to the seasonal fluctuations can be a key reason for success.

Business Cycles

Within the economy there are business cycles. These cycles vary in their duration and intensity, but include a number of prominent phases. In the expansionary portion of the cycle, production and spending levels increase and unemployment levels fall. Businesses generally prosper and bankruptcies are minimal. This culminates in a "peak" when the economy is functioning at its best levels before a "contraction" begins. This contraction can result in either a recession or depression, depending on the contraction's severity. During this phase, spending, production, and profit levels fall, and unemployment and bankruptcies increase. The base of this period is called a "trough," before expansion begins anew.

Numerous factors can induce the waves of expansion and contraction. Some of these factors include: the government's economic and monetary policies, inventory levels, and people's expectations.

It is important for the businessperson to prepare for the contractionary phase of the business cycle when times are good. This will help to ensure that the business survives thorough difficult times to enjoy the benefits of the next recovery.

Graph 2-1

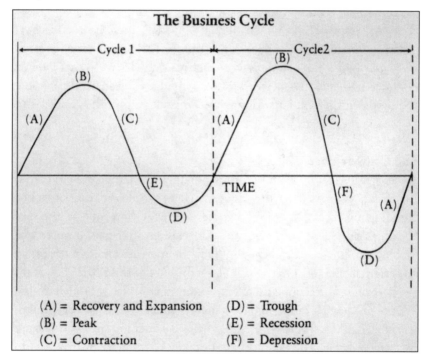

The Business Cycle

(A) = Recovery and Expansion   (D) = Trough
(B) = Peak   (E) = Recession
(C) = Contraction   (F) = Depression

Product Life Cycle

The third major cycle to consider is the product life cycle. Products go through four phases within this cycle: introduction to the marketplace; growth; maturity; and decline. Each of these stages is associated with certain events and business strategies.

Introduction to the Marketplace

A new product entered in the marketplace will either have to create a demand or serve the needs of "pent-up" demand, which is demand that exists but is currently not being serviced. Sales in this initial stage are usually slow, while production costs are quite high because of a lack of economies of scale and technological problems that are encountered with producing a new product. For these reasons, the product price is usually quite high, and the lack of competitors in this introduction stage allows the price to remain that way.

A good strategy often adopted in this stage is a "high profile-high price" approach. This can be useful to capture a substantial portion of the marketplace, establish brand-name leadership, and discourage competition. Some firms opt for a "low profile-low price" approach, in which they attempt to gain consumer acceptance as quickly as possible. If this latter strategy is used, it often works best if the marketplace is highly price-elastic, so that a lower price will lead to a disproportionate change in quantity demanded. (For a further explanation of "price-elasticity" see the "Four P's of Marketing" section.)

The Growth Stage

If the product finds and satisfies a market need, then demand often increases swiftly. In this stage of growth, sales increase quickly, allowing economies of scale to be realized. Often though, the savings realized by the economies of scale are not passed on to the consumer, but instead the firm uses the increased margin to recoup original costs or simply obtain larger profits. If this is the case, competitors are encouraged to enter the marketplace, often refining the product to carve their own market niche. As growth continues, new market segments (see "Market Segmentation" section) are targeted, with the establishment of new channels of distribution to reach the consumer.

The Maturity Stage

The maturity stage contains three subsections. First, sales continue to grow but at a reduced rate. During "saturation," the market has reached its potential, with the vast majority of customers being repeat purchasers. In the third subsection, "decaying maturity," sales levels begin to drop. This can lead to industry over-capacity which results in increased competition as businesses battle for a shrinking market. Both price and promotional competition usually intensify during this latter output phase. This competition usually pressures some businesses to reduce output or vacate the field, while other firms are forced into bankruptcy.

The Decline Stage

During the decline stage, sales decrease, companies withdraw from the market, and promotional budgets are usually reduced. Operators that stay in the field can sometimes be rewarded by increased sales as they gain clients from firms who have left the industry. Depending on the product or service though, it is possible that demand might completely disappear.

To avoid the decline stage, firms often try various strategies to prolong the growth period or lengthen the period of maturity. One method frequently utilized is "market modification." Market modification is a search for new market segments that might potentially buy your product, or a repositioning of the product so that increased usage will result from existing buyers. For example: by convincing the public that eggs are not just for breakfast, but also ideal as a dinner, the egg advertisers are attempting to reposition eggs within the marketplace.

"Product modification" is another technique utilized to avoid a decaying marketplace. Here, the product is changed so that people are convinced that is "new and improved," "stronger," "more powerful," or a host of other wonderful and silly sundry adjectives that advertising presents. Consumers often believe these messages to be important, and product sales avoid the decline.

As you evaluate your product or service, it is important that consideration be given to its place within the product life cycle, as this will affect both the sales and marketing strategy. In the majority of cases, new entrepreneurs start a venture in a field that is in a growing or a mature market. Few novice businesspeople have the resources or the knowledge to bring a new product or service into he market. Markets in decline should be avoided. Pity the businessperson who opened a plant producing slide rules, as the calculator was introduced to the masses.

Graph 2-2

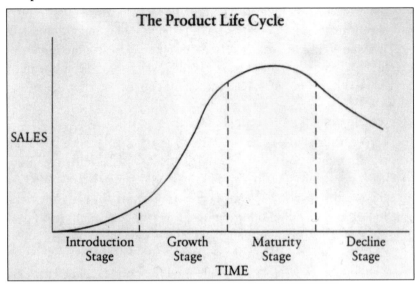

The Product Life Cycle

SALES

| Introduction Stage | Growth Stage | Maturity Stage | Decline Stage |

TIME

What type of Business Organization? Proprietorship*, Partnership, or Corporation

One of the first decisions that you will be faced with is whether to form a proprietorship, a partnership, or a corporation. Each of these organizational models has distinct advantages and, consequently, disadvantages which should be carefully examined before you decide on your business format.

Proprietorship

A proprietorship is a business owned by one person who is legally responsible for all of the business debts and other legal obligations. This means that if the proprietorship incurs debt, the owner is liable to the creditors.

Advantages of a Proprietorship

A) Easy to Start
Hypothetically, you can decide to go into business tomorrow morning: you can hang your shingle on the wall tomorrow after-

---

* Proprietorship — also called a "sole proprietorship."

noon; pat yourself on the back tomorrow night; and say, "Congratulations, I am now an entrepreneur." Of course, this is one of the quickest methods of joining the eighty percent business failure casualty list. Still, you will have the memories of the hours that you were a businessperson. Seriously though, a proprietorship is that easy to start. You do not even have to register the business with the government if you operate the venture under your own name.

B) Low Start-Up Costs

If you do register your business with the government, and it is advisable to do so as registering a business helps to create the aura, if not the reality, of professionalism, you will discover that the start-up fees are extremely low. Also, prior to registration, you should do a "name search" to make certain that your prospective business will not have the same title as an existing organization. If you do not do the name search and you have taken another business's name, the danger exists that at a later date, you will be forced to change the title of your organization, which can be a costly undertaking. The cost of the name search is extremely low.

C) Personal Incentive and Profits

The sole proprietor makes all of the decisions and reaps all of the profits of the business enterprise. This helps to create tremendous personal incentive.

D) Freedom and Speed of Action

Since the owner does make all the decisions, he can act quickly, without conferring with his colleagues or partners. He also has the freedom to utilize skills that might be ignored if he worked for another organization — skills that might lead to increased job enjoyment.

E) Potential Tax Advantages

Proprietorship do present the opportunity for their own distinct tax advantages and disadvantages. Remember, it is perfectly legal to practise tax avoidance, but it is not legal to practise tax evasion.

F) Limited Regulation

The government demands minimal report keeping from sole proprietorships. This factor can save a tremendous amount of time and expense.

G) Ease of Dissolution

Remember the shingle that you hung on your wall yesterday? Well, today you have decided to close the business. As long as there are no creditors chasing you, you can just pat yourself on the back and say, "Congratulations, I am no longer an entrepreneur."

Disadvantages of a Proprietorship

A) Unlimited Liability

By the definition of a sole proprietorship, the proprietor is legally responsible for all of the business debts and other legal obligations incurred by the enterprise. This liability means that if the business does poorly, creditors can claim your house, your car, and any other assets that you possess, even if these assets are distinct from the operation. This liability is a major consideration when you choose proprietorship status.

B) Difficult to Raise Capital

Usually the more people involved in starting an enterprise, the more capital that is available. A sole proprietor, therefore, will have the most difficulty in raising funds for the operation.

C) Lack of Continuity

If the owner of the business becomes sick or dies, odds are that the business will close. Proprietorship status often does not allow for the continuance of an enterprise, even a successful one.

D) Limited Talent

As one advantage of a proprietorship, it was mentioned that the owner can utilize various skills — skills that might be ignored if she worked for another organization. The flip side of this is that often the owner will be forced to rely upon herself in areas in which her abilities are lacking, a reliance that might seriously harm the endeavour.

E) Stress

The proprietor has all of the responsibilities for the business. The long hours necessary to establish a new enterprise, or simply the pressures that build when the operation is facing difficulties can easily lead to stress. This stress may result in poor health, and a business dependent on one individual may be forced to close its doors.

F) Possible Heavier Taxation

It is useful to compare the personal and corporate tax structure to see which is most advantageous. Once again, an accountant can prove to be extremely useful in helping analyze this situation.

Partnership (See also Appendix IV)

A partnership exists when two or more persons combine their funds and abilities to carry on a business for profit. There are two kinds of partnerships to be considered.

A) General Partnership

This is a partnership in which all of the partners share in the management of the business and have unlimited liability for any losses incurred.

B) Limited Partnership

This is a partnership in which some of the partners have limited liability to their investment in the partnership, but at least one partner will retain unlimited liability. It is important to note that a limited partner will become a general partner if he has a hand in management.

Advantages of a Partnership

Many of these advantages are the same as with a proprietorship, and therefore, relate directly to the corporate status. Partnerships are started simply by registration with the government, and the start-up costs can be extremely low. Personal incentive remains great, although it is sometimes tempered if the partners start to bicker. Tax treatment is on the personal income tax statement, and this should be compared with corporate rates when choosing the organizational type. A broader management base can be critical for the success of a small business, making the formation of a partnership ideal, as the various individuals involved utilize their specialized skills. An excellent mix might occur if one person is a top-notch salesperson and marketer, while the other partner takes care of the financial side of the operation. As was highlighted in the major reasons that small businesses fail section, sufficient capital is critical for a new ventures success. A proprietorship might not be able to provide sufficient capital to operate a business. For this reason, a partnership may be more viable. Lastly, as with a proprietorship, government regulation of a partnership is extremely limited.

Disadvantages of a Partnership

A) Unlimited Liability

As with a proprietorship, unlimited liability is often considered to be the major disadvantage of a partnership. Once again, creditors can attempt to claim your house, car, or other assets, for debts owed by the partnership. In addition to the unlimited personal liability of the proprietorship, you are also saddled with individual, joint, and several liability. This means that you are responsible for the debts incurred by your business partner(s), unless you are a limited partner. For this reason, among many others, partners must be chosen carefully.

B) Difficulty Raising Capital

Though capital is easier to raise than in a proprietorship, a corporation often has access to greater amounts of financing.

C) Lack of Continuity

When a partner dies or leaves the business, the partnership is dissolved, even if the other partners wish the operation to continue in an identical manner. The business can remain intact, however, if the remaining partners or a new partner agree to form a new partnership. It should also be noted that one individual cannot sell his position to an outside investor without his partner's consent.

D) Possible Heavier Taxation

Once again, a comparison with the corporate tax structure must be made to see which form of organization is most beneficial.

E) Relatively Frozen Asset

In the proprietorship situation, you could decide immediately to close your office door, pay off your creditors, take the rest of the money out of the business, and leave on a vacation for Honolulu. In a partnership, it is not necessarily that easy. Sometimes, if difficulties exist between the partners, or by the stipulations of the partnership agreement, it can take years before money is retrieved from the business, making the investment a relatively frozen asset.

F) Divided Authority

In the proprietorship, the owner could act quickly without consent from other individuals. In the partnership situation, quick action is not always possible, and these delays in action can be caused by disagreements.

G) Hard Finding Suitable Partners

Forming a partnership is akin, in many ways, to forming a marriage. Often, it is easy to find a partner. The difficulty is finding a suitable partner for the long-term. If you make a mistake, it can prove extremely costly in terms of money, time, and stress, so it is wise that you take time to find the "right person."

H) The "I Hate You!" Syndrome

This is a label I have given to an extremely common occurrence. In the beginning, you and your partner — be it your best friend, wife, or whoever — get along swimmingly. But gradually, a falling-out occurs, until finally, you literally hate each other. This happens again and again, in partnership after partnership.

To help alleviate the difficulties in both operating and dissolving the enterprise, it is extremely wise to prepare a "Partnership

Agreement" before you enter business together. This agreement should demonstrate what the partners expect from each other, and also how the company will be divided if this occurrence becomes reality. By placing in writing at the beginning of the relationship — when parties are at their most reasonable — the activities that will take place at the end of the relationship, you will ultimately save all of the involved parties a great deal of ill will, bitterness, and time at the "divorce" proceedings. A lawyer is a virtual necessity in the creation of this partnership agreement.

The Corporation

A corporation is an intangible being, invisible, and existing only in contemplation of the law. It is a legal entity, having a continuous existence apart from that of its owners.

"What does that mean exactly?" you might be asking. It indicates that the act of incorporation creates something completely new, a being that is responsible for itself. I compare it to giving birth — a completely new entity is formed that must ultimately be responsible for itself, as it is separate from the parents. This is different from either a proprietorship or partnership, which are identified as a legal part of the owner. A corporation is distinct from the owner; therefore considered a being unto itself.

Advantages of a Corporation

A) Limited Liability

This is usually considered the most important reason to incorporate. Since a corporation is its own being, debts incurred by the corporation are the responsibility of the business rather than the owners. This means that unless you agree to use your home, car, or other assets as collateral for the venture, even if the corporation goes bankrupt, you can retain these items.

The situation sometimes is a bit of a Catch-22 though. Often, even though you have incorporated, your friendly neighbourhood banker or other financial aid will not lend you funds unless you personally guarantee them. In this case, you are in the same position as if you had formed a proprietorship or partnership. To avoid this situation, you must negotiate as skilfully as possible, attempting to limit the amount of your personal assets being secured as collateral for the loan.

B) Easier to Raise Capital

A corporation has access to larger pools of capital than the other forms of business. The stock market is the most notable financing tool open to corporations attempting to raise funds.

C) Specialized Management

When people consider a corporation, they normally think of a large organization with a marketing whiz, accountant, salesperson, and various other experts. This means specialized management for the organization.

This is not always the case. A corporation can actually be operated by one person; in this instance, management would not be more specialized than in a proprietorship. But in a larger corporation, specialization is definitely a positive element.

D) Ownership is Transferable

To change ownership, shareholders can sell their holding in the corporation. The corporate status remains unchanged by this event as the business is considered an entity unto itself.

E) Potential Tax Advantages

Corporations are taxed at various rates, which are often preferable to personal tax levels. This tax advantage is usually even more important to small companies, as different government levels sometimes create special tax deductions for these businesses, making incorporation even more attractive. (See "Tax" section.)

F) Continuous Existence

The corporation is an entity with a life all of its own. If the shareholders of the corporation die, the corporation continues as the heirs decree.

Disadvantages of a Corporation

A) Expensive to Start

Regardless of the method chosen, starting a corporation will cost at least hundreds of dollars. The majority of people choose — and usually with good reason — to engage the services of a lawyer for the act of incorporation. The use of a lawyer increases the start-up costs even more, therefore, incorporation is often not feasible for many starting a small business, as the money saved can be used in the working capital of the operation.

B) Closely Regulated

Government regulations are quite extensive for corporations. Many small business people find that complying with all of the government's stipulations is an onerous process, which takes a great deal of time. This is further complicated if the corporation is going to operate in more than one province. In this case, with a few exceptions, a federal charter is needed, which means that the company has to comply with both federal and provincial regulations. It is recommended, therefore, that if a business is to be operated in only one province, whenever possible, only a provincial charter should be obtained.

C) Extensive Record-Keeping

To comply with the extensive government regulations previously mentioned and to satisfy the needs of shareholders, extensive record-keeping by the business is a necessity. Such record-keeping takes time and is often quite costly.

D) Double Taxation

Double taxation occurs when the corporation pays taxes on profits, and then the individual receiving dividends from the business must also pay taxes on earnings. This double payment can be a disadvantage of the corporate set-up.

Before starting your business, carefully evaluate the pros and cons of proprietorships, partnerships, and corporations; then decide which business form would be most advantageous for your organization. Remember to consider both short- and long-term needs when making this decision.

It is possible to switch from one business type to another, and this is often done for tax reasons. This strategy is outlined in the "Tax" chapter.

Chart 2-1

Comparison Chart of Proprietorships, Partnerships & Corporations		
	Advantages	Disadvantages
Proprietorship	A. Easy to Start B. Low Start-Up Costs C. Personal Incentive & Profits D. Freedom and Speed of Action E. Potential Tax Advantages F. Limited Regulation G. Ease of Dissolution	A. Unlimited Liability B. Difficult to Raise Capital C. Lack of Continuity D. Limited Talent E. Stress F. Possible Heavier Taxation
Partnership	A. Easy to Start B. Low Start-Up Costs C. Personal Incentive D. Additional Sources of Capital E. Broader Management Base F. Limited Regulation G. Potential Tax Advantages	A. Unlimited Liability B. Difficulty Raising Capital C. Lack of Continuity D. Possible Heavier Taxation E. Relatively Frozen Asset F. Divided Authority G. Hard Finding Suitable Partners H. The "I Hate You!" Syndrome
Corporation	A. Limited Liability B. Easier to Raise Capital C. Specialized Management D. Ownership is Transferable E. Potential Tax Advantages F. Continuous Existence	A. Expensive to Start B. Closely Regulated C. Extensive Record-Keeping D. Double Taxation

But Where Will I Obtain the Money?
Financing the Business

Adequate capital to both commence and operate the business until the cash flow situation becomes positive is a necessity for a successful operation. A substantial number of businesses never realize a positive cash flow, often because they only obtain enough money to set up the venture, but not enough to operate the enterprise. The cash flow analysis will indicate the amount of funding that is necessary for the operation to survive and it is hoped, flourish. But where will you obtain the funding?

When potential lenders or investors analyze whether or not they wish to participate in your operation, odds are that they will consider the "Four C's of Credit": Capacity to Repay, Capital, Character, and Business Conditions.

Capacity to repay will depend on whether or not the business can generate the necessary cash to satisfy the lending requirements in a specified period of time. The terms of the agreement can base the financing on short- or long-term needs, with various payback periods, defined for both the principal and the interest. The projected financial statements for the business will indicate the capacity to repay.

The capital invested by the owner will help to indicate whether he is committed to the business, and whether there is a willingness to assume a substantial portion of the risk. This commitment is important to lenders or investors, as they want to know that the owner is intent on making the enterprise a success.

The character of the borrower will be assessed in both a personal interview, and by an evaluation of the business plan that is presented. Sometimes, financial assistance can be found for a venture that is not considered completely financially sound, because the financiers believe in the character of the owner and his ability to make the operation a success.

Lastly, business conditions often have a major impact on the granting of financial assistance. During the oil boom days of the new millennium, funding was extremely easy to obtain for the oil patch. But gradually, as oil prices dropped, the bloom came off the rose and business conditions dictated that oil exploration was not the ideal market for investment. Funding in this area, therefore, was greatly reduced as a consequence of changing business conditions. But still the question arises: Where should you look for funding?

A) Yourself

It is to be hoped you will have some capital to invest in the business because, as stated previously, without personal financing other monetary sources will likely give your financing proposal short shrift. The greater your level of investment as a percentage of the capitalization of the business, the more independence you will have as the importance of funding from investors and lenders will diminish. In addition to the degree of independence enjoyed, usually the more personal equity as compared to debt equity in the operation, the better the chance for business success.

B) Family and Friends

Some professional advisors scorn this type of financing, as the result can be family disputes and broken friendships. To avoid such disputes, specify as dearly as possible the terms of the financing (often this is preferential to market rates), and make certain that family and friends recognize who will be making the decisions for the business. Sometimes it is best that family and friends have no decision-making authority, while in other situations, relying on those you are close to for advice, motivation and inspiration can often insure business success.

C) The Small Business Loans Act

Under this act's directive, loans at a rate of prime (the rate that banks give to their best customers), plus one percent, are available to new and existing small businesses whose gross revenues are less than two million dollars. Eligibility for these loans depends on being involved in: the retail trade, a service, construction, communications, manufacturing, wholesale, or transport. The business is allowed to have a maximum of $100,000 outstanding at any time under the loan agreement, and this money can be used to purchase premises, equipment, or land, or to modernize the business. Loans are not available for working capital purposes under this programme. The maximum payback period for these loans is ten years, and the loans must be secured either by a first charge on equipment, the premises, or with a mortgage. Banks or trust companies and a few other lending agencies administer these loans.

D) Commercial Banks

Banks are prime lenders for small business. They will be interested in seeing a well-prepared business plan, collateral guarantees, an investment on your part, and a business-like approach to the operation that shows you want to make the venture a success. Rates and terms at the different banks can vary, so shop around.

E) Credit Unions

Credit unions were originally established to serve their union membership, but anyone who makes a deposit with them can now become a member. Gradually, these unions have become more sophisticated in their loan operations, but they are generally willing to accommodate most members whose business has the potential to benefit the community. The lending limits of the various credit unions vary tremendously depending on their size, but they are authorized to lend money under the Small Business Loans Act, as are the federal banks.

F) Trade Credit

Suppliers will usually grant payment terms that will help to finance the inventory that the business needs. Credit terms are often for 30 or 60 days. As the business grows and establishes a track record, the line of credit might be increased: an amount that could be particularly substantial for a small firm doing business with a number of suppliers. This credit is essentially an interest-free loan. Often, it is worthwhile to take trade discounts, as such discounts can present a substantial savings from paying the full invoice. An example of such a saving scheme is: 1%, 10 days, net 30, which means that if you pay within ten days you receive a one percent discount; otherwise the full amount is expected within thirty days. By taking the discount an annualized saving of 18 percent is achieved: a very substantial saving.

G) Venture Capital

Venture capitalists have been a rapidly growing major source of financing in the past few years. Usually, venture capitalists will provide equity in exchange for a percentage of the business. Essentially then, they become your partners — usually with a minority interest

— and often they are extremely active in helping to operate the business. The expertise offered can prove to be extremely positive for the operation, but some owners dislike this interference in the affairs of "their" business. Venture capitalists also usually invest in businesses with the potential for dramatic growth. This desire to be involved only in high-growth companies can be self-defeating for business owners who truly wish to remain small, but become partners with a venture capitalist.

H) Government Programmes

All levels of government have programmes which provide financing to small business operators. Among other areas, these programmes can help to buy equipment, hire employees, renovate premises, and export your product. (See "Government" section.) Gradually, the government is becoming more businesslike in its approach to financing ventures — a positive step for the proper usage of tax dollars.

I) Partners

Sometimes the easiest way to raise additional capital, and to obtain talent at the same time, is to take on a partner. Having a partner is an extremely popular method of increasing the capital base, spreading responsibility for the business, and perhaps allowing family and/or friends to work together. Of course, as mentioned in the section on partnerships, numerous disadvantages exist in this arrangement. Because of the drawbacks of working with associates, a partnership agreement should be carefully considered.

J) Share Offerings

Selling shares on the stock exchanges as a public company is standard technique for generating enormous amounts of cash while maintaining operating control of the company. Many potential share offerings are rejected, and the preparation and approval time to obtain a listing is both lengthy and rigorous, two factors that discourage a number of individuals. An alternative to public stock sales is a placement of shares. In this case an investment dealer offers preference shares in the business to individuals who are given a priority on future dividends, but who receive no voting power for their investment.

K) Insurance Companies

Insurance companies will sometimes give long-term loans, usually in return for mortgages on real estate. Generally, these companies do not engage in short-term financing.

L) Finance Companies

Finance companies will also lend money to small business people. Many of these loans are for equipment and machinery and the payback schedule is usually precise.

Obtaining money for your enterprise consists of "shopping" and negotiating for the best financing arrangement. Take your time, when looking for funding, for once you are locked into an agreement, it is often very difficult to disengage yourself. Remember also that if you can finance the complete venture yourself, then you will not have to respond to lenders or investors, and greater independence is a worthwhile consideration for an entrepreneur.

Chart 2-2

Funding Options

A) Yourself	G) Venture Capital
B) Family and Friends	H) Government
C) The Small Business	Programmes
Loans Act	I) Partners
D) Commercial Banks	J) Share Offerings
E) Credit Unions	K) Insurance Companies
F) Trade Credit	L) Finance Companies

TIME MANAGEMENT

Time management has become a major growth field in the past decade, as businesses attempt to utilize time more effectively. By doing this, money, energy, and of course, time itself are saved. By following a few axioms, you will be practising some of the essentials of time management.

Parkinson's Rule

Work expands to fill the time available for its completion.

Set realistic deadlines when establishing the time limits for assignments. This applies not only when you are delegating work to employees but also when you are setting deadlines for yourself. Certainly, everyone is familiar with the situation in which an assignment is due in six weeks, and almost inevitably, the last few days are spent scrambling to complete the job, because the previous five and a half weeks were underutilized. By setting realistic deadlines, more will be accomplished.

Pareto's Law

The law of the vital few and the trivial many.

Pareto, a mathematician by trade, arrived at this law, perhaps, after noticing that many individuals have a tendency to attempt the trivial first, and in the process, become bogged down in unimportant detail. Ultimately, this allows less time for the most important jobs. The application of this law dictates that tasks should be prioritized the most important tasks being distinguished from those of lesser importance. Next, concentrate on completing the tasks of greatest significance, before moving on to other items. By doing this, you will avoid the problem of concentrating too long on trivial pursuits, then finding that time is lacking for the major chores.

Think, then act.

Simple logic, but certainly there is often a tendency to ignore this one. Do not attempt to act quickly or impulsively, before focusing on the act that you wish to accomplish; otherwise you might respond like the proverbial chicken: darting madly about but accomplishing little. By planning, focusing on your goals and objectives, far more can be achieved. The potential danger in this maxim is that some individuals think "forever" and never get around to the act. This is often the case with people who have a viable business idea, think it through completely; but then ponder some more, rather than acting. In this case, and many other similar situations, the time to act is now.

Never touch a piece of paper more than once.

The key element to gain from this message is to avoid the continuous reshuffling of papers to which many individuals are prone. It is common for some people to work from a bin, starting at the top chore and working to the bottom. Often though, there is a tendency for certain jobs to be continually recycled, as unfavourable tasks surface, only to be shuffled once again to the bottom of the pile. The time taken to consider these items, before they are rearranged in the pile, is often enough time to make a large dent in the task.

Murphy's Law

If anything can possibly go wrong, it will.

This has become one of the most popular laws in the past few years. If something does go wrong, do not just sit back and become depressed as you do nothing. Act accordingly, if the situation can be corrected, and if the task is impossible, then move on to something new that can be completed. Certainly this is easier said than done, but be realistic. Many difficulties are going to present themselves as you commence and operate your business, and the better prepared you are to cope with these problems and to push ahead, the more efficiently you will work.

CRITICAL PATH SCHEDULING

Critical path scheduling is a worthwhile concept to understand and apply. The essence of this technique is that for a certain event to occur, a necessary sequence of events must precede it. For example, if you wish to open a store, some events that might be necessary before you open include: renovating the premises; hiring employees; and ordering, receiving, and stocking inventory. Let's say that you decide to lease the store on August 1, planning to open on November 1 to take advantage of the Christmas business that represents 55 percent of your trade. The contractor says that he will be finished October 15, which appears to be perfect, as that gives you two weeks to train employees and stock the shelves. The critical path then looks like this:

August 1	*October 7*	*October 15*	*November 1*
Lease the store. Renovations begin.	Employee interviews.	Renovations finish. Employees start. Inventory arrives. Shelf stocking begins.	Doors open.

In this critical path, the renovations must be finished before the employees can start stocking the shelves, and this must be completed before the store will be ready for customers. These events are contingent upon each other. If the renovations are delayed, which is often the case, being finished on November 15 instead of October 15, then approximately one month of sales might be lost, as the store will not be able to open until December 1. If renovations are delayed until December 1, then the store will open even later, and the bulk of the Christmas sales — the major season for this enterprise — will have been lost. Such losses could prove disastrous for the venture, and could potentially lead to bankruptcy if funds are not available to supplement the cash position.

It is wise to prepare a critical path schedule to forecast the major events that will affect your business. If one event is contingent upon another, sometimes a time "lag" between activities will ensure that the process can be completed on time. This additional time might prove valuable for the business to meet its deadlines and obligations, and therefore to be a success.

FACTORS AFFECTING SALES

Before estimating sales projections, it is important to understand the major factors that affect sales. These factors are best divided into two sections: external factors, which are factors over which you have no control, and internal factors, which are those factors that can be varied to affect sales.

External Factors

Though external factors are beyond your control, you can often analyse the future so that trends can be predicted. Prediction of these trends can help to choose a good business to enter, and can also help you to fulfil future consumer requirements that will increase sales.

A) Natural Events

Natural events can have a tremendous impact on a business's sales level. One of the most obvious natural events is weather. If you sell skis, and the winter is warm and virtually devoid of snow, odds are that your sales level will tumble. On the flip side, if you have a summer food stand, and the weather is balmy every day, sales should blossom.

B) War

War can have an impact on sales levels in numerous industries, causing the demand for products in various fields to expand rapidly, while other areas will be forced to curtail trade. The spin-off effect, which is the impact on industries not directly affected by the war, but still experiencing a change in demand because of the impact on other industries or consumers, can also have an effect.

C) Government Policy Changes

The government can alter the tax structure; change the policy for imports, which might increase or decrease the competitiveness of your market; vary pollution control standards; change the bank rate; or alter one of numerous other policies; and these changes can have an impact on your sales.

D) Size and Age Composition of the Population

The Canadian population is aging. This means that there is a growing demand for nursing homes; medical facilities; drugs and various other products; and services for the elderly. At the same time, Canadians are having fewer children per capita, changing the nature of the children's marketplace. When entering a business, you should attempt to foresee future trends, and from these predictions you should try to estimate future demand.

E) Incomes

As the wealth of the population increases, discretionary income also rises. This trend allows for the purchase of more luxury goods, such as fur coats, while the purchase of necessities, such as bread, will remain fairly constant. Often the change in per capita income level is partially a result of government policy.

F) Change in the Price of Substitutes

Substitutes are goods that can be utilized in the place of other goods. For example: if the price of apples skyrockets, people might choose to substitute for them by eating more pears. As a pear farmer, therefore, your sales will increase. The converse for this also holds true, for if the price of a substitute decreases, then odds are that your sales will also drop.

G) Change in the Price of Complements

Complements are goods that are used jointly with other commodities. For example, say that you own a store that sells stereo speakers. If the price of tuners and amplifiers drops dramatically, more people should purchase your speakers. But if the price of tuners and amplifiers rises precipitously, then speaker sales should abate.

H) Expectations

When people believe that times ahead will be good, they tend to buy more. When the future is full of doom and gloom, people often save money for the rainy days, and decide to postpone purchases.

Internal Factors

One of the major reasons why businesses fail is a lack of sales; therefore, to create additional sales, you must carefully evaluate the best method of influencing internal factors.

A) Price

In economics, an area of analysis exists called "elasticity of pricing." (See marketing section on "Price.") Essentially, elasticity of pricing is the change in demand for the product or service, as a result of a change in price. Understanding this concept can aid in setting the best price for a product or service, thereby insuring sales levels that will maximize profits.

B) Advertising

Advertising creates knowledge and awareness of a product, and knowledge and awareness help to generate sales. Naturally, people cannot buy products or services about which they have no information. Both the quality and quantity of your advertising will directly affect your sales levels.

C) Employees

Your employees must present a certain image that is compatible with your product or service. They should also be motivated and trained to do the best possible sales job for the business. This can have a tremendous impact on the profit level of the venture.

D) Salesmanship

Often in small businesses, the owner is the only salesperson; therefore, your level of salesmanship must be excellent if you are in this position. If, as the owner, you cannot sell your product, then the business will probably experience major difficulties. Often, a key reason that people return to a store is because the owner and staff are knowledgeable. Providing expertise is a portion of salesmanship that is a key success variable for many enterprises.

E) Location

Where to situate your business is one of the first decisions you will have to make when you set up a venture. Choosing a good location can affect your sales dramatically. (See "Choosing Your Location" section.)

F) Layout

Store layout and presentation of the products will have a major impact on sales. Some stores prefer the cluttered, "Look around and you are sure to find what you need" atmosphere. Other stores present more spacious, sophisticated surroundings. Many outlets rely, for a large proportion of sales, on "point-of-purchase" displays — displays mounted where the customers pay for their goods. These point-of-purchase displays can lead to substantial "impulse" buying, as people purchase items on a whim. This can increase profits substantially. Certainly the product or service sold dictates the set-up to a large degree, but it is critical that maximum care is taken to create an optimal layout. (See "Layout" section.)

G) Costs

Though costs are dictated by suppliers to a large degree, skilful negotiation can help to greatly reduce costs, which in turn can allow a reduction in price for the consumer. This will enhance the competitive position of the business and should increase sales.

H) Product or Service

The quality of the product or service will have a major impact on sales. In addition to this, the packaging, the guarantee, and a number of other factors will affect the public's acceptance of the product or service.

Careful analysis of both internal and external factors will enable you to make educated business decisions. This will help the business to thrive as an action plan is implemented from these decisions to optimize sales and, therefore, profits.

PREDICTING SALES

One of the major reasons a business fails is inadequate sales. It is crucial, therefore, that before commencing a venture, you estimate as accurately as possible, the sales volume your business will achieve, to see if this sales level will make your operation viable. To estimate the sales level, numerous sources and methods are at your disposal, some of which are listed below.

A) Check with Potential Buyers

Approach your prospective customers. See if they do, indeed, desire the product or service you propose to offer. If possible, obtain their signatures on a contract, thereby guaranteeing yourself a specific level of sales. This will help reduce failure.

B) Check with Suppliers

Your potential suppliers will have excellent knowledge about the nature of the marketplace: whether it is expanding or contracting; short-term versus long-term trends; the ability of newcomers to survive; and a wealth of other information. The possibility exists that suppliers will paint the marketplace in glowing terms, in the hope that you will become their customer and expand their sales; therefore, a limited dose of skepticism might prove beneficial here. However, usually suppliers are an excellent source of information.

C) Check the Competition

Naturally, this will not be as easy as walking into the competitor's location and saying, "Hi! I propose to be the new boy on the block! How's business?" But by spending time at the competition's location as an interested consumer, numerous questions about the state of the industry and, therefore, future sales levels can be answered.

D) Market Research

Market research can be an excellent tool in helping to estimate sales. Be careful here though. Some of the firms utilize shoddy research techniques; often you would be better to create the survey instrument; implementing and analysing the results yourself. Remember, to do a proper survey, it helps dramatically if the individuals doing the work have an understanding of the industry. This will allow them to ask the correct questions and categorize the responses more accurately.

E) Trade Journals, Business Publications and Newspapers

All of these publications will have some information that is relevant to your sales prediction. Recent articles in your field can be found easily at the library by checking in periodical listings such as, "The Reader's Guide to Periodical Literature," and the "Business Periodicals Index" under your industry area.

F) Libraries

Libraries are loaded with information that will prove extremely helpful. Some of this data will provide detailed market information by analyzing your sector and predicting future trends. In addition to this, libraries can provide you with useful information on all facets of commencing a new venture, from a historical perspective to the most recent technological advances.

G) Boards of Trade

Numerous Boards of Trade publish and store all types of data including: analysing trends in industry; changing population demographics for specific regions; regional per capita income; and numerous other vital statistics. Also, the Board of Trade might be able to recommend local sources that could aid your business.

H) Marketing Reports

Various organizations, such as *The Financial Post*, Dunn and Bradstreet, and Moody's compile information on various industries. Some of this information covers consumer marketing data; major events in specific fields; a competitive sectoral analysis; and predicted sales patterns.

I) Government Publications

Most of us wonder where our tax dollars are going and how we can possibly benefit from their expenditure. Well, one place that the money disappears is to numerous government periodicals, many of which can be useful when starting your venture. Some of the best data to help you estimate your sales is provided by Statistics Canada, which has done surveys on both population and industry. Other government information is available through various government offices and the library.

J) Experience

Experience is the key to estimating sales, just as it is the key ingredient in starting a successful enterprise. Previous experience in the business arena of your choice will give you inside information on your sales potential, on the marketplace, on the competition, and on many other facets of the operation.

K) The Internet

Last, but only because it is most recent, is the Internet. This is one of the handiest places to seek out all kinds of information, as you can sit in the comfort of your home, wearing only pyjamas, and no one will be the wiser. In addition, as more and more people log on, the quality, and quantity, of data is increasing drastically. Of course, as with many things in life, one has to sift through the dross to arrive at the jewels.

Checklist 2-1

SALES PREDICTION CHECKLIST	YES	NO

A. Have you checked with potential buyers?
B. Have you contacted suppliers?
C. Have you scouted the competition?
D. Have you done some market research?
E. Have you checked trade journals, business publications/and newspapers?
F. Have you utilized the library?
G. Have you contacted the local Board of Trade?
H. Have you checked various marketing reports?
I. Have you utilized government publications?
J. Do you have the experience to predict future sales? If not, how can you obtain this experience?
K. Have you scoured the Internet?

Have you also carefully considered:

External Factors	Yes	No

A) Natural Events
B) War
C) Government Policy Changes
D) Size and Age Composition of the Population

E) Incomes
F) Change in the Price of Substitutes
G) Change in the Price of Complements
H) Expectations

Internal Factors	Yes	No

A) Price
B) Advertising
C) Employees
D) Salesmanship
E) Location
F) Layout
G) Costs
H) Product or Service

The greater number of these areas checked "Yes," the better will be your estimate of future sales.

CASE 2: HOT DOGS!!!

Steve Berger was broke. He had recently been fired from his job at The Photo Booth after being late for the sixth time in a month, and he was debating what to do next. He knew that he had seen enough pictures for a lifetime in his seven weeks at the store, and wanted a job far away from the photographic world.

Steve was not discouraged about his future though, because ski season was rapidly approaching and he loved skiing. He also knew that at 23 years of age, he had lots of plans and ideas ahead of him. His foremost thought was to start a mobile hot dog stand on a bike cart. Steve was certain that the old town of Montreal was an ideal location for this business, as tourists and local workers loved hot dogs. Steve had observed this himself.

When Steve talked to his father about borrowing $3,000 from him, his father being of the "old school," suggested that Steve should earn the money himself, and then start the business. "Too much time involved for that idea," Steve thought to himself.

Steve then approached some of his friends for financing the hot dog venture. Three of them agreed it was a great idea, and each agreed to take a 17 percent interest in the business for $1,000 per person. Steve's friends particularly liked the idea of how he planned to incorporate the business so that they could all save money on their taxes and limit their liability. "Don't want to have to pay some jerk if a hot dog gets stuck in his throat," Steve told his friends with a laugh.

Three days later, the partners paid their money. Steve then went to see a lawyer who incorporated the business for $1,000. After that, he bought a bike cart and cooking gear for $1,500. He then went and purchased a vendor's permit, before buying $250 worth of inventory. Steve was happy as he still had a few dollars left, and the day was a sunny 59 degrees, perfect for business. Steve set up at a major intersection, and sold his full stock within four hours for a profit of over $200.

What do you think of Steve's chances for success?

PART III

COST-BENEFIT ANALYSIS

One area that must be considered by the businessperson is cost-benefit analysis. Cost-benefit analysis, as the name implies, is the consideration of the costs of a decision as compared to the benefits received. The costs and benefits are not always of a monetary nature and this can make the calculations more difficult.

Every day consumers use this technique. Typical cost-benefit decisions for a consumer include: Should I buy a dishwasher for $750 or do the dishes by hand? Should I spend $100 to see a hockey game or spend the money somewhere else? Should I buy a house that is close to work downtown or pay less for a larger home in the suburbs?

Government must also constantly evaluate different cost-benefit relationships such as: the cost-benefit results of increasing or lowering taxes; raising or lowering the bank rate; raising welfare payments; or reducing tariffs for importers.

For the businessperson, cost-benefit analysis is of continuous importance. For example: you might be considering hiring an employee to do all sorts of general and menial tasks that you don't wish to do. The basic cost of the employee is the wage package that he receives, plus the time that you or other employees spend training him. The benefits that will be received include: the employee's productivity; additional time for you to do other tasks that will bring in larger amounts of income; and perhaps the enjoyment of avoiding work that you detest. Initially, when the enterprise is started, hiring an employee might be too large an expense, even though the perceived benefits appear attractive. Later on though, as the operation expands and the cash flow situation improves, hiring an employee may become more feasible.

Another major cost-benefit decision that often must be made is whether to lease or buy equipment. Both of these options have specific advantages. By leasing equipment, risk is reduced, as the owner will normally be responsible for all repairs. In addition to this, a business that has limited funds will be able to spread payments over time, which can greatly enhance the cash flow position. (See "Planning Your Cash Flow.") But leasing can also be very expensive, as the costs continue to mount, usually on a weekly or monthly basis. In addition to this, unless there is a purchase agreement involved, the business never acquires the equipment, for which it has continually been paying.

Some other cost-benefit decisions you might make include: whether to purchase a brand name computer or a clone; whether or not to locate in a higher rent district with a greater traffic flow; and whether or not the credit lines of certain customers should be increased. Through correct decision-making utilizing this technique, your chance for business success will be greatly enhanced.

RISK AND INSURANCE

Risk

Risk generally means damage, injury, or loss. For the entrepreneur, risk is usually in the form of a potential financial loss. By recognizing the potential for loss, the businessperson can take the appropriate actions to counteract the situation. This is done as part of the financial decision-making process.

The best method of identifying the risks associated with a business is to examine the different assets and operations used, and then to estimate the loss in view of potential difficulties. This examination will likely include a number of the following areas that present risks for small businesses.

A) Damage to Property

Property consists of the building, equipment, and other assets owned by the business. These assets are constantly in danger from the possibility of fire, storm damage, or other problems. This area presents a major risk for most businesses.

B) Theft

Theft is a constant hazard that many businesses must recognize and take action to prevent. It can be the result of people outside the business or employees.

C) Death of Key Employees

Valuable employees are also a major asset for businesses. A loss of a key employee can have severe effects on the sales and profit levels.

D) Bad Debt Losses

This refers to those uncollectable accounts that can cause financial hardship and potential bankruptcy — often the result of shoddy practices for extending credit.

E) Liability to Employees

Employers are accountable for the safety of their employees, while they are working. This responsibility has been increasing in recent years.

F) Public Liability

Owners are also responsible for the public and sometimes their property, while on the operation's premises. In addition to this, the business is liable for any goods sold to the public.

Coping with Risk

Among a number of different methods of coping with risk, the most common are the following:

A) Avoiding Risk

Though risks can rarely be eliminated completely, often they can be minimized. Methods to do this include: incorporating the venture so that unlimited liability is not a factor; leasing equipment to place the burden of risk on the owner; depositing cash in the bank at the end of every business day to avoid theft; and providing as safe a workplace as possible.

B) Self-Insurance

With this method, businesses set aside a certain amount of funds to be utilized in case of difficulties. This method can be quite effective and cost efficient, but there are two major problems. The firm may have serious difficulties early in its development, and might not have enough funds set aside to meet its needs, leading to the temptation to use funds in a way other than insurance.

C) Co-Insurance

Under this programme a savings plan is adopted by a number of firms in the same industry with the funds to be utilized by any member that faces predefined difficulties. This allows the various businesses involved to share the burden of risk. This technique is quickly gaining in popularity, because of the recent rapid increase in insurance rates.

D) Transferring Risk

This is the most common technique of minimizing risk. Under this plan, the business can transfer risk to an outside agency for a fee; essentially, trading money today against uncertainty for the future. This is the domain of the insurance agent.

The costs of coping with risk can vary dramatically depending on the method that is chosen. This is a typical example of a cost-benefit decision. Often, business people choose transferring risk as the best method of minimizing potential losses. To transfer risk effectively, a good insurance agent can help.

Finding an Agent

Finding a good insurance agent takes a certain amount of "legwork." Check with friends and business associates and find out who their agents are, and if they are pleased with the service. Often bankers or lawyers can recommend a reputable individual, with whom they feel you will be comfortable. Find an agent who represents your needs, and is not just intent on "insuring" himself a hefty commission.

Often a person who represents a number of insurers can be best. This can reduce the costs of the insurance substantially, as the best insurance is chosen from different companies. The agent should provide information on a number of different policies that will suit your needs and, ideally, be able to provide a package deal, rather than a "piecemeal" insurance plan that includes 42 different companies. Remember that the funds utilized for insurance cannot be invested in another area of the business — an important consideration for a small operation that has limited resources. Be careful that you do not over-insure.

Types of Policies

Numerous policies are available to protect small businesses. Some of the following might apply to your operation:

A) Life Insurance

Life insurance helps to protect the family in case of the death of the breadwinner. There are two types of life insurance: whole life and term. Whole life insurance means that premiums are paid throughout the lifetime of the insured with the whole policy paid upon the insured person's death. Term insurance is a contract for a specified number of years, after which an agreement must be made to continue the policy. Often a business will buy term insurance as one of the benefits for the employees — insurance that can be purchased at a lower rate for the group than if bought individually.

B) Health and Accident Insurance

This insurance helps to guarantee that an employee will be adequately cared for if injured. It is useful to offset the costs of hospitalization and medical attention.

C) Fire Insurance

Fire insurance is bought to protect the assets of the business. Building, equipment, and inventories are all prime considerations when thinking of this kind of insurance.

D) Loss Protection

Loss protection insures against theft or burglary. Insurance related directly to employee theft is particularly expensive to obtain.

E) Comprehensive Liability Insurance

This form of insurance is particularly useful when the product or service is such that personal or business damages are possible. An example of this is a contractor who wants to make certain that he is adequately covered if an employee is hurt on the job site.

F) Automotive Insurance

This form of insurance is identical for both personal and business liability. A prime consideration for a business is the necessity of protecting employees who use company cars.

G) Key Person Insurance

This insurance will protect the company if a key person in the organization dies or is sick for a lengthy period.

H) Business Interruption Insurance

This form of insurance is useful when a business is interrupted by a fire, major accident, or other difficulty. During this period, when the business will not be producing any income, business interruption insurance will cover salaries, fixed expenses, and lost income from sales, until the business recommences operations.

Insurance Terms

When considering buying insurance, it is helpful to understand a number of terms. These include:

1) *Beneficiary* — The person who will receive the value of the policy if the insured person dies.
2) *Cash Value of Policy* — If the policy is such that it can be cancelled, this is the amount that the insurance company will pay upon cancellation.
3) *Face Value of Policy* — This is the amount that will be paid if the insured person dies.
4) *Paid-Up Policy* — The amount of money necessary to keep the policy valid.

Risk is a natural element that must be considered before a business is started and operating. Insurance needs should be assessed at this time, and re-evaluated on an annual basis. This will prove beneficial when difficulties occur.

THE ACCOUNTANT

To decide whether or not to choose an accountant, you should carefully study the resources your business possesses. Is an accountant practical, considering the financial position of your operation? In many cases, especially in the early stages of an enterprise, hiring an accountant is simply not feasible. As the business grows, this may change, and a chartered accountant might become a practical necessity. When this time arrives, you should shop around carefully to find a person with whom you feel comfortable. Often it is worthwhile to find an individual who is in the same age range as you with an office that is close to yours. Also, it is worth considering the size of the accountant's office. Do you want to work with someone from a small operation, so that you will be known? Or would you prefer to hire a major agency, while realizing that sometimes you can, indeed, become lost in the shuffle?

Certainly if you approach the majority of accounting firms, they will assure you that it is necessary for you to obtain their services. Unfortunately, these services do not come cheaply. Most accountants will charge you a fee based on the time they spend on your case, the type of work involved, and the level of staff needed to do the work. The fee for this service can vary between $50 and $250 an hour, with national firms generally charging a higher rate, and smaller firms about twenty percent less.

Many accountants can save you more money than they will charge. A good accountant can help you start your business by showing you proper operational methods of financing and, of course, proper accounting systems with appropriate computer software. In addition to this, once the business is developing, an accountant can help you improve office efficiency, guide you to proper insurance protection, make you aware of government assistance programmes, and help to prepare your tax returns while insuring that you pay the minimum tax required.

Later, as profits accumulate, the accountant can help you maximize your usage of the money, demonstrating different methods of employee compensation.

But remember, these services will not be provided cheaply. To reduce the fees your accountant will charge, do not ask for services that you can do yourself, or that one of your staff can provide less expensively. Give your accountant the maximum assistance possible by providing all of your bookkeeping information. If you are going to have work that must be done in a hurry, give the accountant notice so that she can prepare herself. Also, be honest. Dishonesty with your accountant means that the government will likely receive falsified information. In the long run, this could prove to be dangerous and, of course, it is wrong.

An accountant can prove to be a valuable member of your business team. However, the costs and benefits of hiring this individual must be weighed. It is a mistake to hire an accountant before your business can reasonably afford one but this individual can be a valuable asset.

THE LAWYER

A lawyer is useful to talk to when starting a small business, providing advice that might ultimately save you a good deal of money in a number of the following ways:

1) Aid in choosing the correct legal form the venture should take: be it a proprietorship, partnership, or corporation.
2) Help in drawing up the documentation for the business (i.e. a partnership agreement, incorporation papers).
3) Help in understanding and observing zoning laws and local legal requirements.
4) Aid in conforming with government regulation and record-keeping.
5) Help in developing contracts with landlords, suppliers, customers, etc.
6) Help in understanding and arranging leases.

Legal fees are normal business expenses and, therefore, can be written off on the income statement as such. Still, even though the fees can be claimed as expenses, often small businesses simply cannot afford this money; therefore, when deciding whether or not to hire a lawyer, carefully examine the financial position of the business and the reasons why a lawyer might be necessary. Decide if you can do the work yourself. In many cases, especially for a small business, hiring a lawyer is simply not reasonable. Once again, this is an example of a cost-benefit decision.

Choosing a lawyer is similar to selecting another adviser. Obtain the services of an individual with whom you feel comfortable. Friends and family who have utilized legal services can often recommend a good person, or perhaps your bank manager or the Bar Association can help. Countless numbers of lawyers are listed in the yellow pages, but a personal reference from someone you trust is better than knocking on various and assorted doors.

A recent trend in the legal profession has been for storefront lawyers, discount prices lawyers, and paralegals. In some cases, these services might be sufficient to satisfy your needs.

THE BANKER

Your banker should have a wealth of experience in dealing with all kinds of enterprises. This expertise can be a valuable commodity as you start and operate your venture.

To take advantage of the information the banker has to offer, it is extremely important that the relationship is commenced in a professional manner. Doing this will require that you approach your banker with a certain amount of respect, dress in a manner that suggests you are a reliable business person, and arrive with complete documentation of your business. If any of these ingredients are not in place, many bankers will not consider your desire for funding seriously.

One useful method to help form a relationship with your banker is to invite him to see your operation. This will give the banker a better idea about your venture, and will help him to arrive at financing decisions and potential operational changes that might improve the business. Of course, the banker's role is not that of a consultant, but often, if the correct relationship is formed, the banker will take the time to provide his expertise. In the long run, this is better for the venture, you, and the bank, as it will help to ensure that all parties will prosper.

EMPLOYEES

Good employees are a major asset for a business, and crucial to ensure success. It is not an accident that some owners seem to have a knack for hiring excellent workers and keeping them, while other organizations seem to have a revolving door of employees. Hiring and keeping good employees is a result of smart ownership policies, as management realizes the value of top-notch employees.

Do I Need an Employee?

Hiring an employee is primarily a cost-benefit decision. Within the benefits received from the employee are the needs of the business to hire that employee. For example, an employee is needed if:

- Service levels would not be sufficient without the employee.
- The workload is too great for you to handle on your own.
- You find certain jobs so undesirable that consideration is given to closing the business if you must continually do them.
- Certain expertise that you cannot provide is necessary.

The benefits received from the employee, therefore, are: productivity; the additional time for you to do other tasks that will bring in larger amounts of income; and the enjoyment of avoiding work that you might detest. The costs of the employee are their wage package and the training time.

Often the costs and benefits of hiring the employee must be weighed before the hiring decision is made. In other situations, need dictates that an employee simply must be hired, or the business will not be able to function.

Attracting Good Employees

To attract good employees to your business, a fair wage and benefit package, and the potential to do the work they are interested in, are essential. One of these without the other is rarely enough.

The wage and benefit package that is offered must be competitive within the industry and/or job market. Research might be necessary to decide just what is fair. Some benefits might include: additional vacation time; sick leave; a medical plan; a dental plan; group insurance; special training programmes; and profit sharing. A clean working environment, high safety standards, and limited noise levels are also important benefits.

The ability to do pleasing work that challenges and motivates will also attract people to your firm. Many individuals in the job market, having become bored with their current positions that do not offer growth, are seeking new stimulation that will allow them to assume responsibility. By offering individuals the chance to grow in a position, high quality, motivated employees should be attracted to your firm.

The Hiring Process

Before you hire an employee, make certain that you know exactly what sort of person you want, and the responsibilities the individual will fulfil; this way the person can be matched as perfectly as possible to the position. Once this is done, the next step is advertising.

One of the simplest and least expensive (free actually!) methods to advertise is to place a job order with the Canada Employment Centre. The centre provides a screening process that weeds out unsuitable applicants and gives you a selection of their best-qualified candidates for the position. Other methods to attract talent are newspaper ads; community college and university placement services; or a simple sign in the window. Another more informal method is to ask family, friends, or current employees if they know of an individual who desires a job.

Once the job placement order is completed and you have received responses, the selection process is extremely important. Remember, it is fairly easy to reject an individual during the interview process, but once hired, it is far more difficult to release someone. There are a number of areas to look for in the interview.

1) Work Experience

Does the potential employee have a good work record or did he constantly switch from one position to another? Has he gained work experience that would be valuable for the position? What was the person's level of responsibility in their last position? What were his duties? What were the applicant's major achievements in his past job? Are good work references available? Other references?

2) Education

Does the applicant's level of education match that which is necessary for the job? Does the educational record show discipline and achievement or is it spotty? Was there involvement in any extracurricular activities that might apply to the position?

3) Personality

Does the applicant seem well prepared for the interview? How does he present himself? Will he fit into the dynamics of the business? Does he seem enthusiastic about the prospect of the position? What does the applicant plan to do in the future?

Depending on the nature of the position, a second interview might be worthwhile. Generally, the more money involved, the greater the number of interviews that are arranged with the potential employee. This is because, as the employee's remuneration increases, the costs of making a hiring mistake also grow.

Keeping Employees

Once you have obtained quality employees, the key becomes keeping them. To do this, it is worthwhile to follow a few simple guidelines:

A) Pay Fairly

Employees want to improve their position in life. As economic conditions change, wages must change to meet these conditions. By reviewing salaries every six months, workers who have been doing a good job can be recognized and rewarded for their efforts.

B) Listen and Communicate

One of the major complaints of employees is that they are not listened to by management. This is unfortunate, for by listening, management can learn a tremendous amount about how the business can be improved so that revenues will increase and costs will be reduced. Certainly, grievances will sometimes be aired, but in the majority of cases solving these difficulties will cost little and improve the overall performance of the business. By opening the channels of communication to your employees, you can also help them to understand why certain decisions are being made, and how their efforts are necessary to make the system function more effectively. The better this communication process is between management and labour, the more benefits will be achieved by both parties from the association.

C) Be Consistent

To work for an inconsistent employer is an extremely stressful experience. The inconsistency can create a hesitancy to act within the work force, resulting in employees who will choose inaction as the route of least resistance. The consequences can be a stagnant business with sluggish revenues.

D) Create a Good Work Environment

Usually the better the work environment, the more productive and content the workers. Certain businesses are mandated to work under certain conditions. Some production plants must exist with a certain level of noise, but the minimization of this level and corresponding protective equipment to prevent ill-effects, will go a long way to keeping workers. In an office environment, giving people flexibility in their breaks, access to other people, yet the privacy that is necessary to accomplish their work, will improve both their working conditions and their efficiency. It is also important to avoid the impact of the omnipresent boss, as this often makes employees nervous and therefore unable to work to their capabilities.

E) Build Pride

People want to be proud of their work, to feel that they are doing something worthwhile. Some owners constantly bully their workers, harping on the negative aspects of their performance, without ever accentuating the positive aspects of the employees' labours. By utilizing the skills of diplomacy and constructive, rather than destructive criticism, employees pride can be fostered and better results achieved.

Establishing Policy and Procedure

By setting in place certain policies and procedures, the work atmosphere should function smoothly and a more comfortable environment will be created for all parties. This will enhance communication and reduce uncertainty, two processes that will improve the employer-employee relationship.

The first procedure is to have the employee submit a detailed work application. This will help your screening process immensely, allowing you to focus on the best employee for the job. Make certain that you obtain references from the candidates; check the references and other data included in the application fully. Conduct the interview in a comfortable milieu, one that sets the potential employee at ease. Discuss in detail the employee's history, accomplishments, and his job expectations, knowing this can help greatly if the person joins the organization. Provide the candidate with a complete outline of the responsibilities, the salary that can be expected, and the potential room for advancement within the firm. Also, fully explain the probation period and its duration, if probation is a policy. This period is usually worthwhile to allow evaluation of a newcomer to the organization.

Once hired, an orientation programme for new personnel is useful. Naturally, the position that the employee assumes will have an impact on the duration and the intensity of the training. As the probation period ensues, assess the employee within the working environment. If the employee is not adequate, then the best alternative is to terminate the relationship. Though this will certainly create stress for all concerned, particularly the employee, in the long run it is usually best that dismissal occur quickly, so that he can find work where he will be appreciated. It will also hurt your business and staff morale if you keep a marginal performer.

Reviews of employee performance are also useful. They give the employee feedback on how well duties are being performed, and a chance to communicate any ideas or complaints. This review will act both as a time to "clear the air" and as an opportunity for some mutual patting on the back (especially from the employer to the employee).

Last, reward workers for their performance. If possible, pay better than the competition, as this will help to ensure that you will attract and obtain the best employees. Also, demonstrate that you appreciate the employee's efforts on behalf of the enterprise, showing that good work does not go unnoticed. In turn, this may increase your profit and enhance your business image, both with the public and in the industry.

ENTREPRENEURIAL STYLE

Entrepreneurial style refers to the manner in which the owners conduct themselves. This creates much of the atmosphere in the work place, and is very important when establishing relationships with employees.

Some entrepreneurs feel perfectly comfortable going out with their employees for a beer after work. For other owners, this situation is uncomfortable and a predicament to be avoided. As an employer, you will have to decide which style is best for you: whether you should become actively involved with your employees outside the business setting, or segregate business and social activities. Naturally, this is a personal decision. Neither of these policies is right or wrong, but either policy could be right or wrong for certain people.

Becoming closely involved with employees outside of work presents a number of potential risks. Sometimes, employees lose respect for the owner, or decides because of the "buddy-buddy" relationship that they do not have to work as hard. If an employer appears to favour some workers over others, jealousies can flare in the organization. Any of these situations can lead to difficulties within the business, a situation that becomes more acute when a friend must be fired.

But there are advantages to becoming close to your employees outside of work. Often this establishes another level of rapport that could not be provided in the working environment. This additional rapport might lead the employee to offer recommendations to improve the business that would not otherwise be mentioned, perhaps stimulate the employees to work harder because they like the boss, or simply make the work atmosphere more enjoyable. Often the advantages of a close relationship outweigh the benefits of maintaining distance.

Co-Operative versus Confrontational Style

Some employers and employees feel that if management makes gains, then labour must be losing; if labour makes gains, then management must be losing. This attitude, which is the basis of the confrontational style, treats the management-labour relationship as a "fixed-sum" situation, where the pie can only be sliced in so many pieces, and a greater piece for one means a smaller piece for another.

The co-operative framework suggests that by working together, a bigger pie can be created for both management and labour. In this situation, the framework is not fixed-sum, but the creation of a "greater-sum": a larger pie.

As the owner of the business, you will be establishing policies that will dictate whether the employment situation is of a fixed-sum nature or a greater-sum creation: a co-operative or confrontational framework. Certainly, by working together, a more pleasant, productive working environment can be created. By recognizing this, you can establish a suitable business environment to serve your needs, and the needs of your employees.

THE PAYROLL SYSTEM

Some businesses choose to use a bank, a payroll firm, or a computer for their payroll needs. All of these are viable options, depending on the number of employees and the resources of the business. If you are planning to do the payroll system by hand though, the following is a simple, efficient system adequate for numerous employees.

To begin the payroll system, you should open an "Employer's Account" with Revenue Canada, when you commence operations. This is necessary as you must remit monthly the tax deductions that you have made from employees' salaries. These remissions will include Pension Plan deduction, vacation taxes, unemployment insurance, and medicare. At the end of the year, a T4 slip (TP4 in Quebec) must be provided to each employee.

For keeping track of the payroll on a weekly basis, a "Total Payroll Sheet" and an "Employee Payroll Sheet" are necessary. (Exhibits 3-1 and 3-2). These will help you greatly as you deal with government and bookkeeping.

Exhibit 3-1

Total Payroll Sheet

Employee Names	Gross Earnings	Fed. Tax	Prov. Tax	UIC	Pension	Medicare	Other	Total	Net Earnings
Totals									

Exhibit 3-2

Employee Payroll Sheet

Name:

Date Started:

Address:

Contact Person:

Phone Number:

Social Insurance Number:

Month	Hours S	M	T	W	T	F	S	Pay Rate	Gross	Fed. Tax	Prov. Tax	UIC	Pension	Medicare	Other	Deductions	Total Net Earnings
Jan. 1–7																	
8–14																	
15–21																	
22–28																	
29–31																	
Total																	
Feb. 1–4																	
1–4																	
5–11																	
etc.																	

Max Abramowitz, whose computer expertise far exceeds mine, contributed the following two sections on Computers and Small Business and the Internet and Small Business. A little foreword via Max.

When my mother found out that I was majoring in geography she asked worriedly, "What are you going to do with a geography degree?" I replied, "Doesn't matter mom — I love computers."

Since then, Max has helped corporations like American Express do useful stuff with computers. Currently, he is an independent consultant based in New York.

COMPUTERS AND SMALL BUSINESS

Around twenty-five centuries ago, computerizing your business involved three simple steps:

1. Go to your local abacus dealer.
2. Buy the newest model.
3. Start adding and subtracting.

However, computers have changed significantly in the past two thousand years and so have the questions one needs to ask and the actions one needs to take when computerizing a business.

Before you run out and buy a new computer, you will need to answer several questions to determine if and how to computerize your business. The obvious question to ask is, "How can a computer help my business?" The not so obvious question to ask is, "What value do I gain by computerizing my operation?" More specifically, will computerization increase your productivity? If so, by how much? Will it help you find new and valuable insights? Will you be able to reach customers to whom you would not normally have access? How many more customers will it enable you to reach? By answering these types of questions, you will be able to estimate how much you stand to gain or lose via computerization. Only then will you be able to determine if computerization is worth the expense and, more importantly, the time and the effort.

Despite the ubiquity of computers in modern offices, for many new businesses a computer is not a necessity. In fact, in many cases, trying to computerize all aspects of your business can be an unnecessary expense and complication. Computerization can be an unwelcome distraction from the more important issues of building a new business. On the other hand, if they are well understood and managed, computers can be a tremendous benefit. They can facilitate day-to-day operations, provide a better understanding of how your business is working, and present a more sophisticated, professional company image to your customers and investors.

Many a consultant has become wealthy helping companies determine and measure what value is added for any particular business venture or proposition. If your business needs are complex, you might consider hiring a consultant, who should be able to expertly analyze your needs and help deliver a complete solution including software customization, systems integration, and training. However, instead of paying scads of money to hire a consultant, you can probably answer the questions relating to the computerization of your business yourself, using the tools consultants use: extensive research and common sense.

In the modern world, there are seemingly innumerable sources of information. The granddaddy of them all is still the library, although the Internet is also an excellent source of knowledge, particularly for computers and other technical subjects. If you do not have access to the Internet, many libraries offer free usage and training on how to realize the greatest benefit from this medium. Read as much as you can. Take advantage of consumer reports, business journals, computer trade magazines, and catalogues. Trade magazines and journals focusing on your particular industry are handy, because they often advertise computer products and services specifically designed to fulfill the needs particular to your industry.

Attending trade shows will also give you exposure to vendors of products and services specifically designed for your type of business. Conventions can be pricey if you register for the seminars, but access to the vendor area is often free. Talk to the computer dealers who are available and strike up discussions with people who have gone through the process of computerizing their business. You can never have too much information.

Very often, people unfamiliar with computers get suckered into thinking the computer hardware (i.e. the central processing unit, monitor, printer, etc.) is doing all the work. In truth, the software programs running on the computer hardware are the key to getting things done.

Therefore, software typically determines what type of computer hardware you will need to buy. If everyone in your industry uses one particular software package, most likely, you will need to use it too, and often a particular software program only operates or works best on a specific type of computer. So, when doing your research, focus on the software. Rely on your common sense; if something does not feel right, it probably is not right. The tricky part of common sense is having confidence in your intuition. However, if you know your business, you will know what works for your situation.

Just as the products and services offered by a business vary, so do the requirements for information processing. However, certain applications are common across all businesses because everyone operates in a similar entrepreneurial environment; an investor is an investor and a customer is a customer, no matter what industry. So what can a computer do for you?

Word Processing

No matter how much today's businesses operate by phone or fax, the written word is still the primary currency of business communications. At some point, you will need to produce a report, an invoice, an order, advertising correspondence, a notice, etc. Productivity is increased by having this computerized.

Communications

Since the early 1990s, the growth of the Internet has been phenomenal and seemingly exponential. It is unlikely that this will change. Access to the Internet provides your business with another method of communicating with your customers. Unlike traditional media channels, like print or television, the Internet makes it as easy for a small company to project a sophisticated image as it is for a large one. This is why the Internet is often called the great equalizer.

Additionally, a computer can be used to send and receive faxes. While for some this might be impractical, for others it can mean access to a business tool they could not otherwise justify. If you intend to use your computer as a fax machine, or if you intend to connect to the Internet a lot, you might consider getting a dedicated connection for your computer. This could be a second or third phone line or a high-speed Internet connection, depending on both your needs and the communications services available in your area.

Spreadsheets

Spreadsheets are the original "must-have" application for personal computers. Describing spreadsheets as electronic ledgers or a fancy way to make a table of figures does not quite do them justice. The modern spreadsheet is a truly remarkable application. On a basic level, it enables you to define a relationship between two or more columns of numbers. For a simple calculation, you are probably better off with a calculator or even a pencil and paper, but when number crunching becomes complex or there is a need to modify the inputs of your calculation, the beauty of a spreadsheet becomes readily apparent.

For example, someone is reviewing your business plan and is questioning the estimate on your raw material prices. With a spreadsheet, you can easily explore how a change in your raw material prices will affect your break-even point. Using a spreadsheet to do this sort of "what if?" analysis is extremely useful for financial forecasting. Additionally, all modern spreadsheets allow you to create graphs of your various analyses, converting the dry and often voluminous numerical output into a form that can be understood quickly and easily.

Accounting and Bookkeeping

Keeping the books can be a boring and tedious task, but meticulous records are indispensable for well-controlled operations and smooth relationships with clients, bankers, and the tax office. Consequently, computerized small businesses should cover at least the following functions: accounts payable, accounts receivable, general ledgers, and income statement generation. All of these elements should be found in any decent office accounting package. More sophisticated accounting and bookkeeping applications greatly automate these processes, but these programs can be complicated; consider conferring with an accountant for advice in this area. In addition, since financial records are important, extra provisions should be taken to protect the integrity of your data.

When it comes time to buy the computer, the first thing to consider is where you will buy it. Working with a local dealer will probably cost a bit more money than if you were to purchase a computer via mail order. However, having a good relationship with your computer dealer over the years will, in most cases, more than compensate for the extra cost.

Look for a computer dealer with whom you feel you can build a long-term relationship. Consider stores close to your home or office; this will make servicing much easier. Sales personnel should be knowledgeable about not just the products they sell but also products with similar market positions. Avoid shopping at busy times so the salesperson will be able to give you her full attention. She'll need to, as hopefully you will have arrived with plenty of questions.

Clearly explain your needs and your budget. Ask for a full demonstration. If there is more than one computer within your budget, try to arrange a side-by-side demonstration. Bang on the keyboards (metaphorically): Is the computer comfortable to use? Assess what you like and what you do not. Get an exhibition of the software you think you will need. Try to arrange a time where you can "play" with the software yourself. Experiment with some data from examples you have compiled.

Keep pumping them with questions. Does the software seem flexible? Will it be able to handle future changes in your business, like more employees, changes in tax law, etc.? Will the software grow as your business expands? Is there a manual? Is it written in plain English? Is training available for this software? Will the software allow you to make major changes in the way you do things? Is it beneficial for both the short- and long-term?

Do not worry about whether or not your computer will be out of date in a year. It will be. There is a well-known joke in the computer industry: Your new computer is out of date by the time you take it home from the store. Six months after you buy a computer, you will be able to purchase the same computer for significantly less than you paid and/or you will be able to buy a significantly more powerful computer for the same price. This is the cost of computer innovation moving at the pace we have come to expect.

When buying a computer, plan on it having a useful life of about three to five years. Do not worry about upgrading unless you enjoy mucking about the inside of a computer, trying to upgrade is typically a value-destroying exercise. The speed improvements are marginal, and the cost — while less than that of a new computer — is not much lower. In truth, most computers are more than fast enough for the applications that most people need. Unless you are a gadget hound or feel you must have the fastest computer in town, do not sweat its obsolescence. The space shuttle is powered by pathetic computers by today's standards. The moral is very simple: Your computer will become outdated, but if it works for you and your business, it does not matter! A computer is only obsolete when it can no longer do what you require of it to run your business.

Finally, choosing a computer is a highly personal decision. If you will not be the one primarily responsible for computer operations, it is a good idea to involve the person or persons who will be in charge of this process. Not only might that person have a better idea of the business's needs, but you will also be employing that old axiom: "Two heads are better than one."

Many people find computers intimidating. However, even with all of their complexities, these machines are getting easier and easier to operate. People from as young as three to as old as ninety can use computers with few problems. Learning to use this machine is not a question of intelligence; it is a question of being comfortable and open-minded about learning new ways to operate.

THE INTERNET AND SMALL BUSINESS

The Myth

An Internet business is not subject to the constraints and limitations of a traditional brick and mortar business.

If the above sentiment was expressed near the millennium, the speaker would have been booed off the circuit, tarred and feathered, and turned into a canapé. Back then, bricks and mortar enterprises were deemed passé, three feet planted on their way to six feet under. A fresh paradigm was the order of the day, and those who did not catch the wave were doomed to perish.

Somehow, the "New World Order" of the entrenched dot.com society hit an iceberg and imploded. Ventures that had raised megamillions of dollars with the expectation that they would rake in billions burned through their funding before gagging and spewing in the deep waters of bankruptcy. While many enterprises survive, now it is obvious: just because your business has a significant Internet component does not mean that revenue will magically flow through the ether into your bank account.

What went wrong? The answer is quite simple really: building it does not ensure that people will come. An enterprise that focuses on the Internet still must have a desirable product or service, with adequate marketing to get the word out, and financials that support the operation. In fact, except for the Internet being used as the channel of communication, there is a scant difference between operating an Internet or traditional enterprise. The fundamentals remain the same.

A "pure" Internet business is one in which a majority, if not all aspects of the enterprise is conducted online. This includes engaging and communicating with customers, accepting payments, and most importantly, delivering a product or service online. It is the delivery of products and services over the Internet that distinguishes a true net venture from a traditional brick and mortar operation with an online persona. Examples of pure Internet businesses are: online market places, content delivery businesses, and industry specific portals.

Stage One: Development

Building a website or application is the first step for any online enterprise. The technical decisions made at this point will have a long-term impact on the manner in which the venture will operate. Online applications are not single entities. They are generally collections of different types of software applications integrated together to form a cohesive whole. Most online applications are composed of three distinct components: a web server, an application server, and a database server. These three components can run on single or separate machines. Once people start talking about scalability (the ability to grow a technical infrastructure to meet increased user demand), redundancy (the use of multiple backup servers and components to ensure that if a single element fails the system continues to function) things can get quite complicated and expensive. While is relatively easy to upgrade hardware and bandwidth, compared to expanding a factory, warehouse or store, it is not as easy or inexpensive to port a software infrastructure from one platform to another.

Another issue that must be addressed during the developmental stage is what to outsource. Outsourcing can be an efficient means for building an online business as a small organization will not be able to hire all the expertise required to build a thriving business. A start-up will have to rely on consultants to provide the skill and knowledge necessary to bring their business online. The danger of outsourcing is the difficulty of retaining knowledge. In most cases it is in a company's interest to outsource as much as possible, with one caveat, proprietary intellectual capital, methods and technology should be cultivated in-house without exception.

Projecting a BIG Image

Small businesses, whether traditional or online, tends to adapt more quickly than their larger competition. Bantam Internet businesses also have the additional benefit of being able to project a "BIG" corporate image despite their diminutive operational size. This means that small online business can potentially compete effectively with large companies, as it is difficult to determine the size of a company from a web page. However, it is not as difficult to ascertain the professionalism of an organization from its website. Good graphic design and top-notch copy go a long way.

However, there is a definite place on the Internet for those enterprises who simply want a promotional presence utilizing this medium. It presents an excellent spot to "wave the flag" so to speak shouting, "We're here, come on and check us out."

For example, say Jon Saunders opens his outdoors and sport store and then he mounts his website. Jane Triathlon, looking for a local store, finds his domain. Jane gets a nice message from Jon and a bit of info about his sports shop. Even if he doesn't have on-line ordering, this might entice her to come on down for a visit. It doesn't cost much to do this, and it shows the public that Jon isn't a complete luddite, even if he doesn't want to make a big investment in a site.

Stage Two: Deployment

Location, location, location. This lament is as true for a traditional business as it is for an online business, but for different reasons. One of the fallacies of the Internet is that these outfits have no physical location. A more accurate statement is that online businesses have a smaller physical presence than comparable traditional companies. Most online ventures require offices and need a place to host their servers. Where a traditional business might want a convenient location on a high traffic street, an online operation will want a physically secure hosting facility with reliable electricity, cooling and multiple high-speed connections to the Internet backbone. Space in a good hosting facility can be very expensive, which is why companies spend significantly more money buying or leasing small rack optimized servers versus cheaper tower systems.

For a small company, renting space in a hosting facility will likely be the greatest recurring cost next to employee wages. In addition, a good hosting facility will provide a menu of invaluable services like system backups, outsourced computer management, and security auditing. Locating servers in a good hosting facility is the best way to keep an online business online (sorry couldn't resist).

Stage Three: Operations

Many of the challenges to building an Internet business are similar to the issues facing a traditional business, although the mechanism may be different. For example, both online and tradition businesses must find customers to buy products and services. The Internet provides access to a potentially huge pool of potential clients. There are about 500 million Internet users worldwide with approximately half from English speaking countries. Finding these people and selling to them is much more complicated for an online business than it is for a traditional small business. An advertisement in the neighbourhood paper might be sufficient for the local beanery, but for an Internet venture it would probably be inappropriate and ineffective.

In the initial stages of this technology, simply having a site was often good enough to attract customers. However this medium has advanced quickly. Sites that were decent a few years ago now appear Neolithic. Attracting customers depends on a demonstrable splash that emanates confidence to consumers, is easy to navigate, and makes clear the products or services on offer, so that buyers will plunk down their cash.

Until recently, making payments through Internet sites has been an iffy process. The primary concern has been the uncertainty that the order could be made in a secure fashion. In some respects, this remains a problem, and passing on a credit card number or bank account is a bit like playing Russian roulette. However, this technology has evolved swiftly to protect confidential information.

Stage Four: Repeat

One essential difference between traditional and online businesses is the pace and necessity of innovation. Online ventures must continually find innovative ways to improve upon processes and increase efficiencies. This is the nature of the medium. Once development is complete, systems are deployed, and customers are streaming to your online business, your work still remains incomplete. On the Internet, change is the only constant.

The Internet as a Resource

The net is like having a library full of information about starting the enterprise, keys to keep it going, data about competition, government programs, taxation, etc. Instead of being stalled on the phone listening to sappy elevator music in the queue, questions can be emailed immediately, sometimes with instantaneous responses. Also, forms can be downloaded, and an intercourse established with distant sources that would otherwise be difficult to achieve.

Here are some sources that may help you start and operate your enterprise. There are scads of others, some easily available, while others require a bit of Internet digging.

1. Business Start-up Assistant
    www.bsa.cbsc.org

2. Canada Customs and Revenue Site for Small Business
   www.ccra-adrc.gc.ca/business/
3. Canada Youth Business Foundation
   www.cybf.ca
4. Canada's Business and Consumer Site
   www.strategis.ic.ca
5. Canadian Careers.com
   www.canadiancareers.com
6. Small Business Canada Magazine
   www.smallbusinesscanada.ca
7. Small Business Knowledge Base
   www.bizmove.com

GOVERNMENT: FRIEND OR FOE?

Many owners of small businesses complain about the documentation that is necessary to cope with government regulations, the inability of government to get things done and, of course, taxes. But the fact is the government attempts to encourage the growth of small business. The primary reason for such encouragement is the employment that results. Small business requires a tremendous number of employees, and thereby decreases the unemployment rate. The government views this reduction in a positive light and wishes it to continue. For this reason, all levels of government have established various assistance programmes to aid in the development of the small business sector. These programmes can be divided primarily into five groups: manpower, innovation and technology, expansion, regional growth, and export.

The Manpower Programme

The government is attempting to ensure a trained, employed population and has implemented numerous programmes under the Canadian Jobs Strategy. The Canadian Jobs Strategy is designed to meet the needs of both employers and workers, by ensuring that employers have competent workers, and that workers have jobs. To do this the government has divided the plan into six parts: skill investment, which is designed to retrain employees before they lose work; skill shortages, which trains people in areas where labour skills are lacking; innovations, which is designed to create novel labour-management solutions to difficulties; job entry, to help new entrants to the work force; and community futures, which is designed to help single-industry communities when an economic downturn appears. Various government assistance plans are available in these areas.

Numerous other government programmes exist in the manpower arena. For more information, contact Employment and Immigration Canada or other manpower-related government offices.

Innovation and Technology

Government is becoming increasingly interested in establishing and maintaining the competitive nature of the Canadian economy. To do this, the government recognizes that innovation is extremely important, and various grants, subsidies, and tax breaks have been established in this area.

One method the government is using to stimulate competitiveness is by establishing innovation centres in various parts of the country. These centres will provide research and assistance to help bring new products or services to the market. Usually these centres charge a fee for their work, but this cost is substantially reduced by government subsidies. One such centre that receives subsidies is the following:

The Canadian Innovation Centre
A1 – 490 Dutton Dr.,
Waterloo, Ontario
N2L 6H7
Telephone: 1-800-265-4559
www.innovationcentre.ca

Expansion

Numerous programmes for expansion exist through various government agencies. Many of these plans include loans at favourable rates, primarily to buy or improve facilities or to purchase new equipment. Most of the programmes do not provide funding for working capital purposes, or to open a second or third store. Under the Small Business Loans Act, financing from banks or trust companies can be arranged at prime plus one percent. This lending plan is the direct result of government action. Your local Federal Business Development Bank office will also provide information on the various types of funding available for expansion.

Regional Growth

The government has designed numerous packages to encourage entrepreneurs to set up businesses in high unemployment or disadvantaged areas. Grants and assistance under these programmes are available from various Industrial Regional Development programmes. Cape Breton, Nova Scotia, is one area in Canada that has had and continues to have significant numbers of programmes targeted towards its future growth.

Export

Over two-thirds of the money targeted from government assistance traditionally goes to support Canadian exports. These programmes are designed to spot potential export markets, finance inventory purchases, hire experts, and aid in numerous other ways. A good product or service that has export potential will qualify for many dollars from the government coffers. For further information, contact the Export Development Corporation office in your area. Addresses of regional offices are given in this book.

Rules for Grantmanship

Obtaining government funding can be an arduous process, but by following a few simple rules the funding that you need will be easier to obtain.

Rule 1: Allow More Time Than You Think is Necessary

Generally, the government is slow in completing designated tasks; therefore make certain that sufficient time is budgeted for the government to help you. If the government people say that a certain task will take a month, budget for six weeks to two months before you expect to see the results. If the act is completed in a month, then just be plain thankful.

Rule 2: Research Thoroughly; Be Prepared — You Will Need Documentation

Most government offices are becoming more businesslike in their approach to utilizing the public's taxes — a fact that can only bode well for taxpayers. If you desire government aid, then fully prepare the necessary documentation to demonstrate that your plan will be a success.

Rule 3: Demonstrate Aid is Vital and Viable

The government agency you approach must realize that their funding will help make your plan viable. They also like to see that the aid is vital for completing the project.

Rule 4: Apply With Confidence

You have a good idea. You need help to accomplish your objectives. Demonstrate these points to the appropriate government office. Show them that you can achieve the ends you desire. Confidence is an essential ingredient for the operation of most businesses.

Rule 5: Maintain Contact

As the application for funding is being processed, make certain that you maintain contact. Otherwise, sometimes you become lost in the shuffle, which may lead to delays in action. If government aid is received, stay in touch afterwards. Tell the government contact how things are going, and express appreciation for their help. Such liaison will make it easier to obtain further help in the future. Remember, government officials usually hear far more complaints than thanks. The latter, therefore, is greatly appreciated.

Rule 6: Remember March 31 is the Government Year-End

Knowing this date is important, for it indicates the optimal time to apply for funding. In April, many departments are flush with cash as they receive their annual monies, and some offices cannot allocate the cash quickly enough. So April is often a good time to apply for government aid. Another excellent time to apply is the beginning of February, as various government departments that have not spent all their funding are searching for candidates to help them spend their treasure trove. Many government officials feel that if funds are left in the treasury, then the budget for the following year will be decreased, and a diminished budget is considered to be undesirable.

Rule 7: Programmes Change All the Time

Here today, gone tomorrow, is often the way with government programmes. Currently, there are scads of aid agendas, of which a large number did not exist, or existed in another form, five years ago. Often an old programme is slightly rearranged with an appropriate name change, and hailed with trumpets of promotion for public consumption, before it also is re-titled. It is often worthwhile to check annually for new government programmes, for one might be implemented that can be targeted directly to your business.

OTHER GOVERNMENT RELATED AREAS

Patents

Patents provide protection for an invention or innovation for a period of 17 years, and are available through the government of Canada from the Canadian Patent Office. The cost of applying for a patent is $150 with another $350 being necessary upon approval, plus an additional $4 per page for proposals exceeding 100 pages. The process of obtaining a patent takes about two and a half years from the time your application is accepted.

The patent is good only in Canada. Patents for other countries must be approved by the host country. Foreign patents also must receive approval in Canada. An invention that has been described in a publication, more than two years prior to the receipt of a patent application in Canada, will not be approved in this country.

Protecting the patent is the duty of the patent holder. If another individual or group markets an identical or similar product, any legal action must be pursued by the patent holder, as the government does not interfere in this jurisdiction.

Patent pending indicates that an application for a patent has been filed. The purpose of this is to discourage potential competition from entering the marketplace. It is useful, when filing for a patent to give as complete description as possible to the patent office. This completeness will not only help to insure issuance of the patent but also help to discourage potential competitors.

For further information contact:
Canadian Intellectual Property Office (CIPO)
Industry Canada
Place du Portage I
50 Victoria Street, 2nd Floor
Hull, Quebec K1A 0C9
Email: cipo.contact@ic.gc.ca

Trademarks

A trademark is a drawing, logo, phrase, shape, or symbol used to distinguish the goods or services of one person or group from another. They are good for a period of fifteen years and may be renewed when this time period elapses. As with patents, trademarks are only good in the country of issue, and applications must be made within the host country for approval. The exception to this is a trademark registered and used in a country that is a member of the "International Convention for the Protection of Industrial and Intellectual Property;" for a trademark established in one of these countries is good in all of the member nations.

Registration of a trademark is not a necessity, but is usually a wise decision, as it helps to clarify one product or service from another. The registration fee is $150, with certification costing another $200, and the renewal after fifteen years currently costs $300. The process of obtaining the trademark usually takes about one year; often individuals choose to utilize the services of a "registered trademark agent." The use of such an agent increases the cost of the application.

To register the trademark contact the Register of Trademarks, Consumer and Corporate Affairs Canada, or your local office. Copies of the Trademarks Act and further information can be obtained from:

Canadian Intellectual Property Office (CIPO)
Industry Canada
Place du Portage I
50 Victoria Street, 2nd Floor
Hull, Quebec K1A 0C9
Email: cipo.contact@ic.gc.ca

Industrial Design

Products made by a manufacturing process that have an original shape, pattern, or ornamentation, are eligible for protection provided by the Industrial Design Act. The article cannot be identical or similar to others in the marketplace.

Once the design has been made public in Canada, the registration process must be completed within twelve months. The initial fee is $160 for five years, with another $215 necessary for another five years. The process usually takes about 30 days. Some individuals choose to register the design on their own, but many people take advantage of the services of a "registered patent agent" or attorney. The services of these individuals can also be beneficial if the industrial design is to be sold or licensed.

For further information contact your local office or:
The Industrial Design Office
Place de Portage,
Phase 1
50 Victoria Street
Hull, Quebec K1A 0C9

Copyrights

A copyright protects original artistic or cultural works in the areas of publishing, producing, reproducing, or performing; it is automatically granted in Canada if the creator is a Canadian citizen, British subject, resident of the British Commonwealth, or a citizen to which the Berne Copyright Convention applies. The copyright also covers individuals who are citizens of a country with which Canada has an agreement.

It is not necessary to register a copyright but the process does help to establish ownership. The fee is quite reasonable, payable to the Receiver General of Canada. The creator's copyright is protected for the duration of his life, plus fifty years after his death. Upon the death of the creator, the copyright becomes a part of the estate.

Copyrights can be sold or licensed either completely or partially; often this is done on a geographical basis.

To obtain more information about copyrights, contact your local office or either of the following:

Canadian Intellectual Property Office
Industry Canada
Place du Portage
50 Victoria Street, 2nd Floor
Hull, Quebec K1A 0C9
Website: www.strategis.ic.gc.ca/sc_mrksv/cipo/welcome/
          welcome-e.html

or
Public Works and Government Services Canada
Place du Portage, Phase III
11 Laurier St.
Hull, Quebec K1A 0S5
Tel: 819-997-6363
Website: www.pwgsc.gc.ca/text/generic/contact_us-e.html

GOVERNMENT ADDRESSES

The following are brief explanations, with addresses and/or phone numbers of government offices that might prove useful to you:

Canada Customs and Revenue Agency
Website: www.ccra-adrc.gc.ca/menu-e.html
Tel: 1-800-959-8281

The Canada Customs and Revenue Agency can provide information on taxes and licensing. This is a select list of some of the major offices.

Alberta
220-4th Avenue South East,
Calgary, Alberta T2G 0L1

Suite 10, 9700 Jasper Avenue
Edmonton, Alberta T5J 4C8

British Columbia
1166 West Pender Street
Vancouver, BC V6E 3H8

Manitoba
325 Broadway
Winnipeg, MB R3C 4T4

New Brunswick
771 Main Street
Moncton, NB E1C 1E9

Newfoundland/Labrador
Sir Humphrey Gilbert Building
165 Duckworth Street, P. O. Box 12075,
St. John's NF A1B 4R5

Northwest Territories
Suite 10, 9700 Jasper Avenue
Edmonton, AB T5J 4C8

Nova Scotia
1256 Barrington Street, P. O. Box 638
Halifax, NS B3J

Ontario
333 Laurier Avenue West
Ottawa, ON K1A 0L9

1 Front Street West
Toronto, ON M5J 2X6

Prince Edward Island
161 St. Peters Road, R. Birt Centre, P.O. Box 8500
Charlottetown, PE C1A 8L3

Quebec
305 René-Lévesque Boulevard West,
Montreal, QC H2Z 1A6

165 de la Pointe-aux-Lièvres South,
Quebec, QC G1K 7L3

Saskatchewan
1955 Smith Street
Regina, SK S4P 2N9

Yukon Territories and Northern BC
280 Victoria Street,
Prince George, BC V2L 4X3

Regional Industrial Expansion

The government has set up a number of agencies to provide aid for regional industrial expansion. These outfits can be useful to your enterprise in a number of ways, from demographic information about the area to financing.

Atlantic Canada Opportunities Agency (ACOA)
www.acoa.ca/e/index.html

Canada Economic Development for Quebec Regions
www.dec-ced.gc.ca/en/main.html

Federal Economic Development Initiative for Northern Ontario (Industry Canada)
http://strategis.ic.gc.ca/SSG/fn00800e.html

Western Economic Diversification Canada
www.wd.gc.ca/eng/default.html

Business Development Bank of Canada
www.bdc.ca/bdc/home/

The Development Bank provides financial and management services to small businesses. It acts as a business bank, presents management training seminars, offers an inexpensive counselling service called CASE, and supplies expertise in numerous other areas.

Some of the Development Bank's offices include:

Alberta
Suite 110,
Barclay Centre 444 – 7th Ave. SW
Calgary, AB T2P 0X8
(403) 292-5600

200 First Edmonton Place
10665 Jasper Avenue
Edmonton, AB T5J 3S9
(780) 495-2277

British Columbia
Nanaimo
Suite 100 - 235 Bastion Street
Nanaimo, British Columbia V9R 3A3
(250) 754-0250

BDC Tower Main Floor
One Bentall Centre PO Box 6505 Burrard Street
Vancouver, British Columbia VTX 1V3
(604) 666-7850

Victoria
990 Fort Street
Victoria, British Columbia VSV 3K2
(250) 363-0161

Manitoba
155 Carlton St. Suite 1100
Winnipeg, Manitoba R3C 3H8
(204) 983-7900

New Brunswick
The Barker House
570 Queen St. Suite 504 P.O. Box 754
Fredericton, New Brunswick E3B 5B4
(506) 452-3030

766 Main Street
Moncton, New Brunswick E1C 1E6
(506) 851-6120

53 King Street
Saint John, New Brunswick E2L 1G5
(506) 636-4751

Newfoundland
Fortis Tower
4 Herald Avenue 1st Floor
Cornerbrook, Newfoundland A2H 4B4
(709) 637-4515

Atlantic Place 215 Water
Street Main Floor
St. John's, Newfoundland AIC 5K4
(709) 772-5505

Nova Scotia
Cogswell Tower Suite
1400 Scotia Square
Halifax, Nova Scotia B3J 2Z7
(902) 426-7850

225 Charlotte Street
Sydney, Nova Scotia BIP 1C4
(902) 564-7700

622 Prince St. P.O. Box 1378
Truro, Nova Scotia B2N 5N2
(902) 895-6377

Northwest Territories
4912 - 49th Street
Yellowknife, Northwest Territories XIA 1P3
(867) 873-3565

Ontario
Manulife Place
55 Metcalfe Street,
Ottawa, Ontario K1P 6L5
(613) 995-0234

102-1136 Alloy Drive
Thunder Bay, Ontario P7B 6M9

(807) 346-1795

150 King Street West, Suite 100
Toronto, Ontario M5H 1J9
(416) 952-6094

Prince Edward Island
BDC Place 111 Kent Street
Charlottetown, Prince Edward Island C1A 1N3
(902) 566-7454

Quebec
259 St-Joseph Blvd. Suite 104
Hull, Quebec J8Y 6T1
(819) 953-4038

2525 Daniel-Johnson Suite 100
Laval, Quebec H7T 1S8
(450) 973-6868

5 Place Ville Marie Plaza
Level Suite 12525
Montreal, Quebec H3B 2G2
(514) 496-7966

Saskatchewan
Bank of Canada Building
2220 - 12th Avenue Suite 320
Regina, Saskatchewan S4P 0M8
(306) 780-6478

135 - 21st Street East
Saskatoon, Saskatchewan S7K 0B4
(306) 975-4822

Yukon Territories
2090 A - 2nd Avenue
Whitehorse, Yukon Y1A 1B6

(867) 633-7510

Export Development Corporation (EDC)

The Export Development Corporation provides insurance, financing, and numerous other services to those businesses pursuing an export market. For further information on the EDC write or call:

Head Office
Export Development Corporation
151 O'Connor Street
Ottawa, ON K1A 1K3
Tel: (613) 598-2500
Fax: (613) 237-2690

Regional Offices:

Calgary
Home Oil Tower, Suite 606
324-8th Avenue S.W.
Calgary, Alberta T2P 2Z2
Tel.: (403) 537-9800

Edmonton
10010-106th Street, Suite 905
Edmonton, Alberta TSJ 3L8
Tel.: (780) 702-5233

Halifax
Purdy's Wharf Tower II, Suite 1410
1969 Upper Water Street
Halifax, Nova Scotia B3J 3R7
Tel.: (902) 442-5205

London
Suite 1512
148 Fullerton Street

London, Ontario N6A 5P3
Tel.: (519) 963-5400

Moncton
735 Main Street, Suite 400
Moncton, New Brunswick EIC 1E5
Tel.: (506) 851-6066

Montreal
Suite 4520
800 Victoria Square P.O. Box 124
Tour de la Bourse
Montreal, Quebec H4Z 1C3
Tel.: (514) 908-9200

Ottawa
151 O'Connor Street
Ottawa, Ontario KIA 1K3
Tel.: (613) 597-8523

Quebec City
Suite 1340
2875 Boulevard Laurier
Ste-Foy, Quebec GIV 2M2
Tel.: (418) 266-6130

St. John's
90 O'Leary Avenue
St. John's, Newfoundland AIB 2C7
Tel.: (709) 772-8808

Toronto
Suite 810
150 York Street P.O. Box 810 Toronto, Ontario M5H 3S5
Tel.: (416) 640-7600

Vancouver
One Bentall Centre Suite 1030

505 Burrard Street Box 58
Vancouver, British Columbia V7X 1M5
Tel.: (604) 638-6950

Winnipeg Office Commodity Exchange Tower
360 Main Street, Suite 2075
Winnipeg, Manitoba R3C 3Z3
Tel.: (204) 975-5090

Statistics Canada

Statistics Canada can provide information on consumer price changes, the labour force, Canadian demographics, and numerous other areas that are concerned with and have an impact on business.

Alberta and the Northwest Territories
Pacific Plaza, Suite 900
10909 Jasper Avenue, N.W.
Edmonton, AB T5J 4J3
Toll-free number: 1-800-263-1136 E-mail: prairies.info@statcan.ca

British Columbia and the Yukon Territory
Library Square Office Tower
600-300 West Georgia Street
Vancouver, British Columbia V6B 6C7
Toll-free number: 1-800-263-1136
E-mail: stcvan@statcan.ca

Manitoba
Via Rail building, Suite 200
123 Main Street
Winnipeg, Manitoba R3C 4V9
Toll-free number: 1-800-263-1136
E-mail: prairies.info@statcan.ca

National Capital Region
R.H. Coats Building, Lobby

Holland Avenue
Ottawa, Ontario KIA 0T6
Toll-free number: 1-800-263-1136
E-mail: infostats@statcan.ca

**New Brunswick, Newfoundland and Labrador,
Nova Scotia and Prince Edward Island.**
1741 Brunswick Street
2nd Floor, Box 11
Halifax, Nova Scotia B3J 3X8
Toll-free number: 1-800-263-1136
E-mail: atlantic.info@statcan.ca

Ontario (except the National Capital Region)
Arthur Meighen Building, 10th Floor
25 St. Clair Avenue East
Toronto, Ontario M4T 1M4
Toll-free number: 1-800-263-1136
E-mail: toronto.info@statcan.ca

Quebec and Nunavut
200 René Levesque Blvd. W.
Guy Favreau Complex
4th Floor, East Tower
Montreal, Quebec H2Z 1X4
Toll-free number: 1-800-263-1136
E-mail: infostcmontreal@statcan.ca

Saskatchewan
Park Plaza, Suite 440
2365 Albert Street
Regina, Saskatchewan S4P 4K1
Toll-free number: 1-800-263-1136
E-mail: prairies.info@statcan.ca

Canada Business Service Centres
   www.cbsc.org

Alberta
100, 10237 104 Street NW
Edmonton, Alberta T5J 1B1
1-800-272-9675

British Columbia
601 West Cordova Street
Vancouver, British Columbia V6B 1G1
1-800-667-2272

Manitoba
250-240 Graham Avenue
Winnipeg, Manitoba R3C 0J7
1-800-665-2019

New Brunswick
570 Queen Street
Fredericton, New Brunswick E3B 6Z6
1-800-668-1010

Newfoundland
90 O'Leary Avenue
St. John's, NF AIB 2C7
1-800-668-1010

Northwest Territories
Scotia Centre 8th Floor
P.O. Box 1320
Yellowknife, NT XIA 2L9
Phone: (867) 873-7958
Toll Free 1-800-661-0599

Nova Scotia
1575 Brunswick Street
Halifax, Nova Scotia B3J 2G1
Toll free: 1-800-668-1010

Ontario

110 Lauder Avenue West, Ground Floor
Ottawa, ON K1P 1J1
1-800 567-2345

City Hall, Main Floor
100 Queen Street West
Toronto, ON M5H 2N2
1-800-567-2345

Prince Edward Island
75 Fitzroy Street
P.O. Box 40
Charlottetown, Prince Edward Island C1A 7K2
1-800-668-1010

Quebec
5 Place Ville Marie, Suite 12500
Montreal, Quebec H3B 4Y2
1-800-322-4636

Saskatchewan
122-3rd Avenue Noah
Saskatoon, Saskatchewan S7K 2H6
Toll Free: 1-800-667-4374

Yukon Territories
201-208 Main Street
Whitehorse, Yukon YIA 2A9
Toll Free: 1-800-661-0543

TAXES AND LICENCES (SEE APPENDIX III FOR GST)

Taxes and licences are necessary for the operation of a small business.
For different businesses, various taxes and licences will apply, many of
which are outlined here.

Sales and Excise Tax

The Excise Tax Act states that sales tax and, under certain conditions, excise tax, must be paid on products produced or manufactured in Canada; sold by a licensed wholesaler; or imported into Canada. Some of these items include: wine, jewellery, cars, motorcycles, tobacco, and gasoline. Federal sales tax is applied at 10 percent except on alcohol, tobacco, and wine which is currently taxed at 13 percent. Some construction materials and equipment for buildings are taxed at six percent. Manufacturers who need an excise tax licence, wholesaler's tax licence, or manufacturer's number should visit their District Excise Office. For an outline of the Excise Tax Act, write to:

Canada Customs and Revenue Agency
www.ccra-adrc.gc.ca/menu-e.html
Tel: 1-800-959-8281

Federal Corporation Tax

This tax is payable to Revenue Canada on a monthly basis. The amount of tax varies, depending on the income of the corporation.

Provincial Corporation Tax

This tax is similar to the Federal Tax. The provinces levy this tax on corporations that operate within their boundaries. The rate varies from province to province.

Personal Income Tax

Federal and personal income taxes are payable together, based on the personal income tax level of the individual. Following the requirements of the Income Tax Act, any person who resides in Canada for over 182 days per year, is eligible to pay personal income tax on income earned both within the country and outside of Canada.

Provincial Sales Tax

Retailers must keep records to show taxable income and non-taxable sales. This is the government levy on the sale of goods sold, used, or consumed in the province. Provincial sales tax rates vary, but all vendors should obtain a licence or registration certificate. This tax is based on the retail price of most goods, some services, and entertainment.

Source Deductions

All businesses must deduct Unemployment Insurance premiums, Canada Pension Plan contributions, and income tax, from their employees' wages. The necessary form and instructions are available from the District Taxation Offices of Revenue Canada.

Capital Gains Tax

Government has a tendency to play with the Capital Gains Tax and change it every few years. Currently for corporations, the simplest way of calculating what to pay is to follow the Schedule 6, the Summary of Disposition of Capital Property. This does become a bit more complicated when dealing with the $500,000 capital gains exemption for capital gains and small business. Individuals should check out the Schedule 3 for this information.

Gasoline Tax and Licences

Every province levies a tax on gasoline although in specific cases refunds are available. This tax is collected directly from the customer by the retailer or service station. In most provinces, the retailers do require a special permit. Importers, refiners, distributors, and others who handle the gasoline, require a licence.

Tobacco Tax and Licences

Tobacco and tobacco products are subject to the excise duty tax. A vendor's permit is necessary under the Retail Sales Tax Act. Any person who is selling cigarettes or other tobacco products is deemed as a wholesaler and will need a wholesaler dealer's permit.

Alcoholic Beverages and Products

With just a few exceptions, alcohol and related products are subject to the excise tax. All of the retail outlets must be licensed. Brewers and distillers need a provincial licence. Manufacturers also need a licence which they can obtain from any district Regional Excise Office.

Bonded Warehouses and Bonded Manufacturers

A manufacturer in bond is an individual who received alcoholic goods and products, such as perfumes, vinegars, and medicines, at preferred rates. The bonded warehouse is where these goods are stored in bond and subject to excise tax. Goods that are transferred from one bonded warehouse to another escape paying additional excise duties. The Regional Director of Excise reviews all the bond applications.

Amusement Tax

In many provinces, a licence is required for certain amusement functions. Often the various cities or towns also have a special tax which they apply to entertainment activities.

Import/Export

For certain goods or commodities to be imported or exported, special permits are needed under the Export and Import Permits Act. For some items no licences are necessary. Specific items are also only exportable under certain quotas, and the importation of some items is restricted. For those importing goods into Canada on a regular basis, an importer's number is suggested. For further information contact the following:

Department of Foreign Affairs and International Trade
Tower C, 4th Floor
L.B. Pearson Bldg.
125 Sussex Drive
Ottawa, ON K1A 0G2
Tel: (613) 996-2387
Website: www.dfait-maeci.gc.ca/~eicb/general/general-e.htm

Delivery and Transport Licences

Depending on the type of truck, and the nature and distance of the haul, different licences are needed. For example, any trucks crossing interprovincial or international lines will require a class X licence. For further information, contact your local transport office.

Municipal Licences

Many municipalities require certain licences for goods sold within their jurisdiction. These licences can range in cost from a few dollars to thousands of dollars, depending on the nature of the work. Also, many municipalities have various by-laws and zoning regulations that must be complied with. For further information, visit your local government office.

Food Regulations

For those dealing with food products, and requiring information in this area, contact your local Health and Welfare Office or:

Health Canada
www.hc-sc.gc.ca/

Drugs and Pharmaceuticals

Information in this area is available from your regional office or:

Health Canada
www.hc-sc.gc.ca/

Packaging and Labelling

Information in this area is available from your local office or:

Canadian Intellectual Property Office (CIPO)
Industry Canada
Place du Portage 1
50 Victoria Street, 2nd Floor
Hull, QC K1A 0C9

Other Licences and Registration

There are numerous other occupations and business areas that will require various licences and registration. Some of these include the travel industry; real estate brokers; business brokers; paperback and periodical distributors; and motor vehicle dealers.

To be on the safe side, check with federal, provincial, and municipal governments to make certain that you are complying with their various requirements before you enter the business.

BUSINESS ETHICS
 OR OH! THE TEMPTATION OF IT ALL!

Marks of the Genuine Man

> He believes in himself.
> He speaks the truth.
> He thinks the truth.
> He acts the truth.
> —*Emerson*

The Random House Dictionary of the English Language, College Edition, 1968, defines ethics as: "a system of moral principles." Unfortunately, this system of moral principles is sometimes ignored — especially in the realm of business.

Adam Smith, who is considered to be the father of economics, suggested that an "invisible hand" is guiding business decisions, such as: a businessperson would pursue the public interest as this would ultimately create higher profits. Mr. Smith was setting in place a worthwhile framework but, certainly, the invisible hand does not work perfectly.

One of the primary functions of government is to make the system work more efficiently. Government attempts to do this by ensuring that the needs are being met of as large a percentage of the population as possible. Taxes, guaranteed wages, and regulations to establish a healthy working environment, are a few of the methods that governments utilize to create a more equitable system. Still, even after government action, and the natural activities of the "invisible hand," there are many areas in which the businessperson must establish standards for ethical conduct.

Some of the ethical questions you might face as a business owner include: whether or not to give labour additional wages and/or benefits when profits are good; deciding on the level of training and job security to provide for employees; whether to reduce the number of employees to utilize machinery; the price to set for your product or service; the quality of the product or service itself; the truthfulness of your advertising; and proper treatment of waste disposal.

The decisions you make to answer some of the aforementioned problems will determine whether or not you will choose to act in an ethical manner. Two of the most common sayings heard from individuals are: "If I don't do it, then the other guy will," or "Everybody does it." If the action is unethical, then let them live with their decisions, but this is not a valid reason for you to act in the same manner. Certainly, almost every person knows the difference between right and wrong. The difficulty often arises when the apparent need to compete overrides the business person's sense of morality. Sometimes this fear of not competing or making the sale becomes so great, so disarming, that the answer appears to exist within a morality that is normally considered taboo, but becomes acceptable, "this one time"; often this becomes another time and then another, before becoming normal policy procedure.

One of the best methods for remaining ethically correct is to follow that old adage, "Do unto others as you would have them do unto you." Usually by doing this, by placing the shoe on the other foot so to speak, it becomes easier to recognize the correct actions to take. Naturally, this is not always an easy process, but acting correctly is *not* always easy. Still, by living in an honest and genuine manner, ultimately you will be more highly respected by the public, employees, and by yourself. This will give you a "good name" — a valuable commodity that should help both your personal life and your business to prosper.

In business, as in everyday life, Emerson's words should be lived by. Slight changes make this quote even more appropriate for this book. I hope that Mr. Emerson would approve.

Marks of the Genuine Business Person

1. Belief in self.
2. Speaks the truth.
3. Thinks the truth.
4. Acts the truth.

MINIMIZE THOSE TAXES

Taxation is part of the price of operating a successful business. Through careful tax planning, it is possible to minimize the amount of taxes you will have to pay. To do this, consider utilizing a number of different strategies.

1) Claim All of Your Expenses

Expenses are costs incurred to earn or collect income. The expenses must be reasonable (i.e. annual flights to Hawaii to view a particularly beautiful hardware store do not count as an expense) and be associated with the business. Personal items are not deductible.

Many individuals disregard a number of their deductible expenses because they either do not understand what an expense is, are too lazy to collect and file receipts, or simply because they assume that the expense is insignificant. This is unfortunate, because the inclusion of every expense for business purposes, can increase the profit level of the business significantly. To claim all expenses, it is extremely important that you keep all of your receipts. This is worthwhile even if you just buy $10 worth of stamps for the business. By keeping your receipt and claiming the stamps as an expense, you will ultimately be increasing your profit by the same percentage as the taxation level.

2) Set an Appropriate Year-End

Your personal tax year is January 1 to December 31. But the business year-end can be any time within the year. This can be a tremendous advantage for income tax purposes, as it creates the opportunity to defer taxes. Deferring tax means that tax is paid later, rather than earlier, allowing the business to continue to utilize and earn additional profits on the tax that would have been paid. This can create additional profits at absolutely no cost. An excellent tax technique, therefore, is to defer paying tax for as long as possible, without being penalized by interest or other charges.

Example 1

Assume that a business is started on February 1 and by the end of December the profit is $50,000. If the year-end is chosen as December 31, then the business will pay taxes on $50,000 profit the following April, when the first tax payment will be due. But if instead of December 31, the following January 31 is chosen as the year-end, the business will not have to pay taxes until April of the following year. By doing this, therefore, you have deferred the tax payment for one full year, which allows the business to earn income on the tax that would have been paid one year earlier.

	Business Start-Up	Year-End Chosen	Tax Payment
Scenario A	February 1, 2002	December 31, 2002	April 30, 2003
Scenario B	February 1, 2002	January 31, 2003	April 30, 2004

Once the year-end is chosen, the business should stick with that year-end unless there is a major reason to change. The government views with suspicion firms that continually vary their year-ends.

Example 2

Assume that you leave your job in September, from which you have earned $25,000 in that calendar year, and you commence your own business in October. Probabilities dictate that your business will be losing money initially; therefore, if the business has lost $10,000 before the end of the year, it might pay to make your year-end December 31 of that year, rather than waiting until the following year for the business year-end. This will lower your effective taxes payable for the first year of operation, allowing you to keep more money that can be utilized for other purposes.

Business Start-Up
October 1, 2002

Personal Income
$25,000

Business Income
Loss ($10,000)

	Year-End Chosen	Tax Payment April 30, 2003
Scenario A	December 31, 2002	$25,000–10,000 = $15,000 Therefore the tax payment is based on $15,000
Scenario B	September 30, 2003	Tax payment based on $25,000

The tax payment in the second situation, therefore, is much higher than the payment in scenario A.

This situation could occur in either a proprietorship or partnership, as the income from the business appears as part of the personal income tax statement. The example would not occur with a corporation because, as was described earlier in the book, a corporation is a separate entity, and therefore must pay tax itself.

3) Proprietorship, Partnership, or Corporation

One consideration in determining whether a proprietorship or partnership, versus a corporation, is more beneficial is the answer to the following question: Can I offset personal income with business losses and therefore lower my overall tax rate? Because businesses usually lose money in the first two years, this offsetting income often makes it beneficial to form a proprietorship or partnership. As time passes though, the business should begin to show a profit, and then a comparison of the personal tax rate versus the corporate tax rate will become important. In rare cases, the business immediately will be a moneymaker, and then the tax consideration is simply which rate is preferable: the personal assessment or the corporate assessment.

In some provinces, an additional consideration in the proprietorship and partnership, versus corporation, decision is the tax holiday for small business. Because of this, it often pays to wait until profits are being made before incorporating. For example: the tax holiday in Ontario allows for a ten percent reduction in tax for the first three years of a small business corporation's life. This circumstance can increase the importance of delaying incorporation until the business is making a profit, to take full advantage of this benefit.

4) Small Business Deduction

As was mentioned in the previous section, in certain provinces there are Small Business Deductions (i.e. the Ontario tax holiday). To remain eligible for these deductions, the corporation often must earn less than a specified amount. Since salaries reduce income, often it is worthwhile to pay salaries to reduce the business income, so that the enterprise will qualify for the Small Business Deduction. An additional aside to this might be that the dividends will be taxed at a preferable rate — another consideration when attempting to reduce taxes.

Some entrepreneurs brag about how their business continues to lose money by manipulation, but remember, the purpose of being in business is to make a profit, not to offset other income. The government will be distrustful of a business that continually loses money but manages to survive.

5) Corporate Income Versus Salary

Another method of limiting taxable income is contingent on the method by which your corporation pays your salary. Often it is worthwhile to limit your salary to the amount necessary to fulfil your needs and desires. This can reduce the tax paid, and increase the amount of money ultimately earned.

Alternatives*	1	2	3
Corporate Income	$200,000	200,000	200,000
Salary from the Corporation	30,000	100,000	200,000
Taxable Income from the Corporation	170,000	100,000	0
Corporate Tax	38,012	22,360	—
Individual Tax	6,587	36,707	81,512
Total Tax	$44,599	$59,067	$81,512

As indicated by this chart, by paying yourself the minimum that you need as in "Alternative 1," the overall tax "bite" is reduced substantially, which can allow for far greater financial returns.

6) Income Splitting

Income splitting is allocating income to the eligible member(s) of the family who will pay the lowest income tax. For example, let's assume that you are currently earning $50,000 and your wife, who is taking a sabbatical from the work force to have and take care of the children, is earning $1,000. By transferring part of your income to her, you can effectively reduce the family's overall tax burden. To do this, your wife must do some work for the business, and she can only be paid fair market value for her efforts. Stipends of $200 an hour for your wife, the bookkeeper, will be considered excessive by Revenue Canada. The same consideration applies if you choose to hire your children.

*there will be a variance from province to province

7) The House or Apartment as an Expense

By working from the home,[*] you can create certain tax write-offs, therefore reducing your income tax assessment. These write-offs can include rent, mortgage interest, heating, insurance, electricity, and others associated with the office. To comply with the government regulations that allow these deductions, the space must be used on a regular and continuous basis for the purpose of earning income; it must be the principal place of business; or must be used on a regular basis for meeting clients.

For example, lawyers, doctors, or accountants, who have an outside office away from the home, cannot utilize any home expenses unless they use the home office exclusively for business, and regularly meet clients at the residence. A university professor with a consulting practice, or a life insurance agent who works exclusively from the home, can take all deductions associated with their office. These deductions cannot exceed the income of the business. If they do, the deductions can be carried forward to subsequent years.

There are two common methods to calculate allowable expenses.

Method 1: Square Footage

If you utilize one room in the home as an office, and the room is 25 percent of the overall square footage of the house, then you can deduct any of the expenses associated with that space, up to a limit of 25 percent of the total home expenses. If the square footage represents 10 percent of the overall space, then a deduction of up to 10 percent would be allowable.

Method 2: Room-by-Room

A similar method often utilized to estimate the amount for deductions is to count the number of rooms in the house. If there are five rooms, and one is utilized as an office, then the deduction would be 20 percent (one room in five) of the expenses associated with the house.

There are two main considerations when calculating this expense. First, what is deemed a room? For example: How many rooms are there in a house with three bedrooms, four bathrooms, a living room, a kitchen, a small den, and an office? Some people might conclude that

*home = apartment for this purpose

for tax purposes there are 11 rooms, while other individuals will calculate six rooms, choosing to ignore the bathrooms and the small den. Which of these tabulations is correct?

The second consideration is whether to use the square footage or the room-by-room method. Imagine a home where the office is one room in five, but only ten percent of the space. By using the room-by-room approach, the taxable benefit would be twice as great as with the square footage technique. Which of these calculations would the tax people accept?

Government tax agents, contrary to some people's opinions, are human; therefore some will consider the six rooms valid, while other agents might insist on any number of rooms up to 11. Some taxation people will allow the room-by-room calculation, while others will insist on the square footage method. The agent's decision could depend largely on your powers of persuasion for the validity of the chosen calculations.

A last factor to be cautious about is depreciating the portion of your home utilized as office space. This is a technique that some individuals choose to use, but difficulties can be created when the house is sold. At this time, the government will deploy a technique called "recapture" to regain the dollars that have been depreciated. An accountant can be useful in advising you here.

As part of your entrepreneurial style, you will have to consider how aggressive you wish to be in pursuing tax deductions. For some entrepreneurs, an aggressive approach leads to nightmares, with midnight visitations by the ghost of Revenue Canada. For others who choose the aggressive approach, the dreams will remain sweet. Assess the type of individual that you are, when considering your tax planning style.

Within the Tax Act, there are numerous grey areas. These grey areas make certain tax deductions potentially reasonable, which allows for various tax strategies, one of which is the aggressive approach. Remember though, there is a major difference between pursuing a grey area deduction as compared to tax evasion. Tax evasion is illegal, Tax avoidance, within the parameters expressed by the law, is legal. This is important to remember, as deductions for your residence, or other tax reduction techniques are considered.

8) Depreciation

Many novice business people forget to include depreciation as an expense. This is a major error, because including this expense will decrease the income level of the business, meaning that there will be less of a tax burden. Depreciation rates vary from item to item. Some of the more common rates include buildings, four percent; machinery and equipment, 20 percent; cars and trucks, 30 percent.

Two common depreciation techniques ordinarily used for calculations are "straight line depreciation" and "sliding scale" depreciation. Straight line depreciation is when a set amount is reduced from the cost of an item on a regular basis. For example, if a piece of machinery cost $10,000 and was to be depreciated at a straight line rate of 20 percent annually, its value after the first year would be $8,000 (20 percent off $10,000); after the second year, $6,000; with a value of zero after five years even though the machinery might still be usable.

The sliding scale method would depreciate the item by a set percentage every year, but this amount would be based on the depreciated value of the asset. For example: a car that cost $10,000 with a depreciation rate of 30 percent would be worth $7,000 after the first year (30 percent off the $10,000). In the second year, the depreciation total would be $2,100 (30 percent of $7,000), making the value of the car $4,900. This pattern would continue.

A good general rule is to depreciate assets as quickly as possible. This is not always the case, as sometimes it proves advantageous to wait until the income level is sufficient before depreciation should commence. It is important that the depreciation timetable you utilize is consistent or Revenue Canada might create difficulties.

9) Maintenance versus Repairs

Repairs are an expense; maintenance is a capital cost allowance. (Capital cost allowance is just depreciation for government purposes.) Because expenses will reduce income more quickly than capital cost allowance, it is worthwhile to designate as much as possible as repairs rather than maintenance so that write-offs will occur more quickly.

10) Telephone Expense

It is quite common for many small businesses that operate from the home to utilize one phone line for both business and pleasure. If this is done, then no deduction is allowed for the telephone, but write-offs are still allowed for long distance telephone calls that are made for the purpose of business.

11) Tax Exemption Numbers

Make certain that you receive the appropriate tax exemption number. This depends on whether the business is classified as wholesale or retail. Receiving this number will help to ensure that you do not pay taxes on goods that you buy. If you neglect to obtain a tax exemption your costs will be higher, making you less competitive.

12) Meals and Entertainment

Meals and entertainment deductions used to be 100 percent, way back in those generous 1987 days, but today they are 50 percent. Exceptions to this rule include restaurants, hotels, and flights deemed as an "ordinary cost of business"; meals or expenses that benefit a registered charity, for which a 100 percent deduction is acceptable; and expenses construed as a benefit for employees and appear on the employees' T4 slips. The employee can then claim 80 percent of this as a deduction with the business writing off 100 percent.

13) Car Expenses

As with other expenses, motor vehicle expenses can only be deducted when they are reasonable and you have receipts to support them. The government can be sticklers when it comes to cars and they advise that you keep a record of the total kilometres driven, along with the kilometres specifically to earn business income. This becomes more complex for individuals who use cars for personal and business trips.

For each business trip, list the date, destination, purpose, and the number of kilometres. Make certain that you write down the odometer reading of each vehicle at the start and end of the year and if you change cars during the year, write down the reading at the time you exchange the vehicle.

There are a number of deductible expenses. These include: license and registration fees; insurance; fuel and oil; maintenance and repairs; interest you pay on a loan used to buy the motor vehicle; capital cost allowance; and leasing costs. The capital cost

allowance for a car is 30 percent, and it works on a declining balance. Those using the vehicle for both personal and business reasons might want to prepare a chart like this.

Horatio owns a tropical fish business and has a van that he uses for
the business. He wrote down the following information for the past year.

Kilometres driven to earn business income:	27,000
Total kilometres driven	30,000
Gas and Oil	$2,000
Capital cost allowance	4,200
Insurance	1,200
License and registration fees	100
Maintenance and repairs	500
Total expenses for the van	$8,000

Horatio calculates the expenses he can deduct for his van in the
current year as follows:

$$\frac{27,000 \text{ (business kilometres)} \times \$8,000}{30,000 \text{ (total kilometres)}} = \$7,200$$

14) Expenses Often Overlooked

Some expenses that are often overlooked but should be itemized
and utilized include: bank charges; stamps and stationery; legal and
accounting fees that are incurred to earn or collect income; and
parking charges. If you spend it, then you should be thinking of
writing it off. Ultimately, the more write-offs you make, the greater
your return.

The majority of business people focus on making the sale, but by
also concentrating on reducing or deferring tax payments, substantially increased earnings can result. This does not mean that any illegal
actions should be taken; just that the government's regulation should
be utilized to your maximum benefit.

BUYING AN EXISTING BUSINESS

One alternative to starting a business from scratch is to buy an existing enterprise. This can often prove to be better than commencing an operation, since buying an enterprise presents a number of immediate advantages.

The major advantage of buying a solid business is that it greatly increases the likelihood of success. There are numerous reasons for this which include: existing customers; a proven location; installed method of operation; established cash flow; secured relationships with suppliers; trained employees; and an established name. Essentially, the previous owner will have expended the energy to do all of the planning and establishing of the enterprise, and you will be able to step in when the business is fully operational and successful.

This does not mean that there are not disadvantages associated with buying a business. First, the owner might be selling for reasons that the purchaser cannot recognize — reasons that might make the operation infeasible. The buyer will also be purchasing any ill-will of the existing business, which can limit the customer base, and sometimes, the existing customers are not desirable. If employees are poor, inventory obsolete, or the marketplace shrinking, the enterprise might prove to be a poor investment. In addition to this, sometimes the business's operating practices are outdated, or the equipment has been poorly maintained.

There are three questions, therefore, that you must consider before purchasing a business. The first question is: Why is the owner selling? Second: What is the business worth? Last: What do I plan to do with the business? To answer these questions requires detective work, patience, and planning.

Why is the owner selling? If he has been in business for forty years, is seventy-two years of age and ready for retirement, the logic appears sound. But if the owner started the venture a year ago, and is just tired of the business and wants to try something new, the warning bells should be ringing. Probe further to obtain any potential information as to hidden reasons for selling. If the owner appears evasive in responding, then simply look for another business; if the rationale for selling appears reasonable, then commence examining the business further.

Begin by investigating the overall operation of the business. When you walk into the store or office, do you sense that the business is organized, the current management competent? If this is the case, the place should have a good "feel" to it. If the place does not have a good feel, odds are that this "opportunity" should be avoided.

On a more quantitative level, income statements and balance sheets for the past five years should be analysed. Check over the numbers carefully. An accountant can be useful here. Do not be afraid to be critical. Financial statements can be "doctored" to make conditions appear much better than they are.

Next, check with customers to see if they are happy with the product and service. If a number of disgruntled customers are found, then the value of goodwill may be minimal. Sometimes customers return to the business because of the owner, and you must analyse if this goodwill can be transferred to you. Sometimes, if you are not a member of the community, this proves to be impossible.

Contact suppliers. See if the current owners have been paying their bills on time. If not, perhaps the business is close to failure, or a cash flow crunch might be occurring that will allow for a lower buying price. Talk to employees. Obtain their opinions on the affairs of the business. Often they have tremendous insights about how well the organization is functioning. Disgruntled workers can often be extremely beneficial here. Talking to employees will also help you decide which ones would be worthwhile retaining.

Carefully analyse the equipment and inventory. Make certain that they are not obsolete or damaged, and are valued correctly on the books. Also, you should check with the business's bankers and the Better Business Bureau. Both of these agencies can be extremely helpful. In addition to this, make certain that all leases and contracts are examined carefully, preferably by a lawyer. This will help to ensure that you are not buying a group of contracts that are inappropriate.

Last, evaluate the accounts receivable. Make certain that they are collectable. Purchasing old accounts receivable can prove disastrous. Ratio analysis (see "Ratio Analysis" section) is an excellent analytical tool to utilize here in order to analyse the financial statements.

Valuing The Business

If the business does seem desirable, then its value must be determined.

There are numerous methods for doing this valuation. One of the easiest formulas to use is the book value. This can be derived simply by looking at the balance sheet, and comparing the assets to the liabilities to reach an equity position. An accountant can be helpful here. This is the basis for the sale of many businesses. One difficulty with this method of setting the price is that it does not always indicate potential profits. A business can be worth $100,000 on paper, but may have limited possibilities for earning future income.

Another technique that is often utilized is "Capitalized Earnings as a Basis of Value." With this technique, the past annual profits of the business are analysed, and a selling price is based on their capitalization rate. For example, if the business has been earning an average of $100,000 annually, and a capitalization rate of 20 percent is chosen (this is a common rate), then the selling price of the business would be $500,000, as 100,000 is 20 percent of 500,000. If the business is one where the risk is limited, a lower capitalization might be used. For example: if 10 percent is the chosen capitalization rate with the same average profit of $100,000 then the business would sell for $1,000,000 $100,000 is 10 percent of this price.

Replacement cost is considered in a number of business transactions. In this case, the cost of commencing operations and building them to the level of the business for sale is evaluated. The major flaw in this method is that existing business assets are rarely worth as much as new purchases.

Another technique is to base the business value on the "seller's price." This is not the price the seller is asking, but rather, the price for which you estimate the person would actually sell. This price might be substantially lower than the book value of the business if the buyer needs money, is tired of working so hard, etc.

Whichever valuation technique is chosen, think about what you plan to do with the business if you purchase it. Perhaps current management is behind the times or lazy, and sales and profits are below easily realizable levels. With this in mind, the organization might be extremely undervalued.

When purchasing a business, using any of these techniques, keep in mind the return on investment desired. If the business will cost $250,000, and you want to receive a return on investment of 10 percent, expected profits must be at least $25,000. Sometimes, an enterprise can be purchased, based on its current return on investment, but you recognize that this return can be increased with sound management. Once again, you might be able to buy an undervalued operation.

When valuing the business, take your time. Some buyers become antsy, feeling that once they have "discovered" the operation, they must buy immediately or the opportunity will disappear. Rushing into a purchase often leads to inflated prices or the purchase of a poor operation.

Negotiating

Negotiating a deal is an art. Once you have decided that the business is worth buying, then bartering can commence. By thinking in terms of four values, your negotiations will prove more effective. The first value is the "roof price," which is the maximum that you would be willing to pay for the business. This will take into account what you intend to do with the enterprise. The second value is the "best price," which is what you estimate the business to be worth with current management. Third, the "book value" should be estimated — the firm's worth on paper. Last, the "seller's price" should be calculated, the value that the seller would probably accept.

Often a seller will initially demand a highly inflated amount for the business. Sometimes this is because of greed; at other times because of business sentiment. In either case, your negotiating stance will be helped greatly if you have definitive values placed on the outfit.

Negotiations can entail more than just a dollar figure for the enterprise. Sometimes other factors can be used to sweeten your deal significantly. By stretching payments for the business, your overall cost is lower, because of the time value of money; by making expenses as high as possible and reducing goodwill, your income tax burden will be lightened; by basing the selling price on future sales levels or profits, the risk factor can be considerably reduced; by having the owner train you for a period of time, you can certainly gain experience and sometimes free labour.

Make certain when the deal is negotiated that the owner cannot re-enter the business for a period of not less than five years. Otherwise, he might set up down the street and quickly regain his old customers.

When making the offer, make certain that escape clauses are included in the contract. These clauses can be dependent on finding appropriate financing; dependent on obtaining certain information about the operation; contingent upon signing a new lease; or other factors. The more general the clauses, the easier to reject the deal if it is ultimately deemed not beneficial.

When negotiating, recognize that you have substantial power. Be willing to walk away from the business and search for another. Do not become infatuated with your own desire to buy, and therefore overpay for the enterprise.

Finding the Business

Finding an appropriate business is a job. Checking advertisements in newspapers, magazines, and trade journals can be useful. Talking to bankers, accountants, or real estate brokers can be helpful, as often these people have inside information on businesses that are for sale but are not advertised. Contact individuals in the industry in which you are looking. Sometimes this can lead to a viable business. Retailers, suppliers, customers, or family and friends might have knowledge about an opportunity.

Remember, though, that skepticism is often well-founded when looking to buy a business. Do not be afraid to ask a lot of questions, and if the answers are not forthcoming or appear illogical, do not hesitate to walk away and search for a better opportunity. Otherwise the danger of buying a lemon exists, when you want anything *but* a grocery store.

THE FRANCHISE OPTION

A franchise is simply an agreement that a buyer may sell the product or service to which another party has title. This field has grown swiftly in recent years, as franchises are an extremely effective method of starting a successful business; over 80 percent of franchises are successful, whereas over 80 percent of new businesses do not exist within five years. The major reason for this is that the franchisee is buying a proven formula.

The franchisor is selling two main features to the franchisee: customer recognition and expertise. If you buy a Burger King franchise, you expect that customers will flock to your door because of the name and the accompanying product. You are, therefore, purchasing good-will, which is the reputation that the business has built up over time. In addition to this, Burger King will have provided their expertise so that you will serve the customers both efficiently and effectively. They will train you and your staff; help find a suitable location; set up the location; establish operating policies; and ensure that your financing is sufficient.

Before purchasing a franchise, there are a number of areas to consider. First, recognize that franchisees are not independent business people. Most franchisors have specific regulations that must be followed for every aspect of the business. This dilutes your decision-making authority and forces you to follow a business blueprint. Usually the more established the franchise, the greater number of regulations that are specified. The trade-off then is less independence for a greater chance of success.

Another area to be considered is that the product or service should be compatible with your business desires. Do not attempt to sell hamburgers if you hate being around food. Become involved with a product or service that interests you, rather than one that beckons because of a profit opportunity.

Another major concern is the legitimacy of the franchisor. With the incredible growth in this field, a number of charlatan organizations have appeared selling bogus franchises to earn a quick dollar. It is crucial, therefore, that the franchisor is carefully evaluated before you spend your hard-earned funds. The following are some questions that must be asked before jumping in:

How long has the franchise been in business?
What is the franchisor's reputation?
Have past locations proven to be successful?
What sort of financing plan does the franchisor provide?
Have they shown their financial statements?
Have they made and illustrated sales and profit predictions for your business?
Have they carefully surveyed the market?
Do they help in training, marketing, and inventory control?
What is the supplier arrangement?
What is the investment that must be made?

What royalty payments are required?
What is the advertising agreement?
What is the estimated payback period?
What are your territorial rights?
What competition is there?
What does your lawyer think of the agreement?
Are existing franchisees happy?
What options exist if you wish to sell the franchise?
Is the market or the product growing or shrinking?
What does the franchisor offer that you cannot do on your own?

Ask the franchisor questions until they have satisfied you completely that they are a *bona fide*, successful, operation that offers an excellent choice for your business success. If the franchisor is evasive or unsure of responses, then be extremely cautious.

There are usually a number of conditions under which the franchisor can cancel the contractual agreement. These reasons include: buying inventory from a supplier not specified by the franchisor; not reaching sales targets; poor service; lack of reporting to headquarters; misuse of the business name; and an absentee owner. The contracts often run for a specified time period with specific renewal clauses tailored to past performance.

Franchise fees vary tremendously. To invest in a new franchise may cost as little as a few thousand dollars, while one of the established chains may demand over a million dollars. In addition to this you might have to pay for the location; set-up fees; royalties that sometimes run as high as fifteen percent of revenues; and marketing fees. The terms of the agreement must be carefully scrutinized.

Franchises are a rapidly growing sector of the economy. For the prospective owners, the major trade-off is reduced risk versus reduced autonomy. For many entrepreneurs, this trade-off is worthwhile.

Chart 3-1

Comparison Chart of Business Options		
Starting a Business	**Buying an Existing Business**	**Buying a Franchise**
Independent	Independent	Not Independent
Least Chance for Success	Better Chance for Success	Best Chance for Success
Must Find a Good Location	Location Should be Proven	Location Well-Researched
Must Establish Clientele	Established Clientele	Name Awareness Helps Create Clientele
Must Provide Expertise	Must Provide Expertise	Some Expertise Provided
Freedom to Set Up Operation	Operation Partially Dictated	Operation Dictated
Must Establish Cash Flow	Cash Flow Established	Cash Flow Not Established but Greater Guarantee
Must Create Goodwill	Some Goodwill Established	Some Goodwill Established
Unproven Success Formula	Proven Success Formula	Proven Success Formula

CASE 3: HERBERT'S VARIETY STORE

Herbert Washington was considering entering a new business. He had just sold his variety store in a small town and had decided to move to the big city to begin operations there. Herbert decided to do this primarily because of his children; he felt that the city presented greater opportunities for them.

Before moving, Herbert decided to go on a scouting expedition to find himself an appropriate business. He knew that he wanted to operate another variety store, certain that his skills in this area would hold him in good stead, even in the big city. Herb went to visit a real estate agent to see what kind of store he could buy.

The agent asked Herbert to tell him about his old store. "It's pretty simple," Herbert began with a trace of a snarl. He wanted to buy a variety store, not talk about himself. "I bought the store in Bleekersville. I doubled its sales within two years, and just kept the old engine purring like a kitten. Some of my suppliers didn't exactly like my negotiating methods, but hell, only a few stopped supplying to me. Anyway, what have you got on the market?"

The agent said he had three potential choices. The first was an empty store at the corner of one of the main downtown streets in an area that bordered both the residential and business districts. Herbert could buy the space for $250,000. Another possibility was to take over a small variety store in a residential neighbourhood that had sales of about $375,000 a year. The asking price was $100,000, including the inventory. The existing lease had two years to run with an option for five more years at $1,500 a month. Lastly, the agent knew of a major franchise that had a few territories left in the city. The asking price was $350,000 for a 24-hour operation that usually paid for itself within five years. "I'm not sure how much you are thinking of spending, Mr. Washington," the agent concluded.

"I could afford all of those. But these franchises seem like a different way of doing business. Sure is a quick pay-back on my investment though."

What should Herbert do next?

CASE 4: BARB'S BLUES

It has been two years since Barb opened her successful shoe "Bootique" featuring moderately priced merchandise from a few local distributors. Her success with her trendy styles convinced her to expand into clothes as well, most of which she sells on consignment from local designers. Last year revenues passed the quarter million mark, so Barb added a part-time employee to join the two full-time staff members.

Although the business is doing well, Barb is finding it tougher and tougher to keep track of the details. She hires an accountant at tax time, but does not feel she can afford this service on a monthly basis. Staying on top of the numbers is taking more and more of her time — time she feels she needs to stay on top of a fickle, cyclical market. She negotiated deals with the different designers, and keeping track of their shares of the inventory is turning into a nightmare. As well, since many of her customers are students, she implemented a layaway plan, which is proving difficult to keep track of.

Barb's brother-in-law, who seems to know something about computers, suggests that a small office system is what she needs. But her shopping expedition leaves her in a quandary.

Option 1) The dealer at a chain computer store puts together a package for $6,000 that works for a broad range of small businesses. But the dealer seems to have problems giving explicit answers to her specific problems, noting that someone will be sent by to help set-up the computer and answer questions.

Option 2) A dealer Barb found in the newspaper offers her a clone package guaranteed to be as good as the name brand. He offers only a few software spreadsheet programmes which he will throw in to sweeten the deal. It's all hers for $3,500, and he suggests she hire a consultant for any special stuff.

Option 3) She calls a consultant who approached her a year ago, trying to sell her a package. He comes into the store the next day and sets up a 'turn key' system; then he enthusiastically demos a package that seems to do everything she can imagine. Price: $14,500, but she must decide quickly; his business is brisk.

Option 4) Barb's brother-in-law recommends a small business consultant, who specializes in installing systems for small firms. This consultant does not have a package to sell Barb, but promises to help her to do the shopping after a thorough analysis of her needs. She charges $35 an hour for her time, and estimates it will take a couple of weeks to get Barb set up and fully trained.

What should Barb do next?

PART IV

Quick Tip 1A: If you do not know something — ask. Remember: curiosity is the key to both intelligence and learning.

Quick Tip 1B: If you need something — ask. People are usually happy to be helpful.

Quick Tip 2: Keep a daily journal. This will help you to focus your activities and thereby save you quite a bit of time and energy.

Quick Tip 3A: Do not be afraid to delegate work. Let employees do tasks of importance. This will often lead to new ideas and happier, more responsible workers.

Quick Tip 3B: Often the employee on the floor has a better idea how to do things than the "man in the booth" (owner). For this reason, amongst others, owners should listen carefully to their employees.

Quick Tip 4: Often there is a better, less expensive method of doing something. Do not continue in the same routine because, "It is the way things have always been done." Experiment. Innovate. Select new options and test them out. If they prove infeasible, then re-establish the routine. Even a short change can often be more beneficial than no change at all.

Quick Tip 5A: Banks have all types of free booklets and information for small businesses. Make use of this information.

Quick Tip 5B: Government also has all kinds of free information. Make the rounds of government offices and collect the publications that apply to you.

Quick Tip 6: Read financial publications. Some worthwhile Canadian publications include: *The Financial Post*, the *Globe and Mail* Business Section, *Canadian Business*, and *Small Business* Magazine. From the United States: *Forbes* and *Business Week* can provide valuable information. These publications will keep you informed and abreast of current events.

Quick Tip 7: Lucky 7 handy addresses:

1. *Canadian Business Magazine*
777 Bay Street, 5th Floor
Toronto, ON M5W 1A7
Tel: 1-800-465-0700
www.canadianbusiness.com/index.shtml

2. Canadian Institute of Chartered Accountants
277 Wellington Street West,
Toronto, Ontario MSS 2Y2
Tel: 416-977-3222
www.cica.ca/cica/cicawebsite.nsf/public/homepage

3. Canadian Tax Foundation
Suite 1200
595 Bay Street
Toronto, ON M5G 2N5
Tel: 1-877-733-0283
www.ctf.ca/

4. *The Economist*
25 St. Jame's St.
London, England
SW1A 1H6
www.economist.com

5. *Success Magazine*
733 3rd Ave.
10th Floor
New York, NY 10017
Tel: 919-807-1100
www.successmagazine.com

6. *Forbes*
60 Fifth Ave.
New York, NY 10011
Tel: 212-366-8999
www.forbes.com

7. *Contra the Heard Investment Letter*
42 Rivercrest Ave.
Toronto, ON M6S 4H3
Tel: 416-410-4431
www.contratheheard.com

Quick Tip 8:   Don't rely on one supplier for all your needs, because if supplies are cut off for any reason, you will be in a precarious situation.

COLLECT THOSE ACCOUNTS RECEIVABLE!

Many small businesses fail because they have difficulty collecting their accounts receivable from clientele. Collecting these accounts is critical, as such collection improves the cash flow situation, helps to reduce losses caused by bad debts, and, ultimately, can make a major difference between a substantial loss and an enviable profit. A number of techniques can be utilized to help ensure that you collect a high percentage of your receivables.

First, be extremely careful to whom you give credit. The ideal payment system is the one in which the customer pays cash for any product or service rendered. The greater the percentage of cash received, the less you will have to collect later. Often though, because of the conditions in your industry, credit is mandatory to gain customers. Extend the credit necessary to be competitive, but do not take unnecessary chances.

Once credit has been extended, make certain that you bill the client promptly. The best method of ensuring that bills are paid quickly is to spend fifteen minutes or so at the end of each day, and make certain that all of your clients have been invoiced.

Often it is worthwhile to offer discounts to customers. An example of such a discount is 1 percent, 10 days; net 30. This means that if the client pays within ten days he will receive a one percent discount. Otherwise he must pay, and one hopes, will, within a 30-day time frame. Other options for discounts commonly utilized are 3%, 10 days; net 60 or 2%, 30 days; net 60. The first example is a discount of approximately 21 percent, the second about 24 percent.

But what should you do if the customer still chooses not to pay within the prescribed time frame? Well, the first step is to divide your accounts receivables into a payment table. (Exhibit 4-1). This division will aid you in keeping track of the level of delinquency of the accounts; then, you must apply pressure accordingly. If payment is not received within 30 days, you might send a nice letter stating that perhaps the customer did not receive the bill or perhaps she mislaid it. If payment is not received in another ten days, then a phone call would be appropriate to see why you have not received your funds. Likely, then, the client will pay, but if he does not, another phone call or letter would be appropriate within ten days. If you still do not receive your money, pay the client a visit. If this does not achieve receiving payment, it might be time for a letter from your lawyer. Remember though, once a lawyer becomes involved, the costs to collect an account increase substantially. Later, if you still achieve no results, perhaps a collection agency will have to be employed or further legal action taken. Cost-benefit analysis will help you decide if either of these latter two techniques should be deployed.

Since you are a small firm, you will probably become fairly friendly with most of your major clients. Such relationships can be a major advantage as you attempt to collect on overdue accounts. Utilize this relationship, as friends will tend to pay friends more quickly than individuals they dislike.

When establishing credit terms in the future, it is important that you check the customer's past performance for reliability. If he is, be fair when granting future credit, but be sure not to leave the business in a vulnerable position. Clients whose records are spotty should be cautiously limited in the amount of credit you allow them to have outstanding. Lastly, customers whose records are poor should be allowed to buy your goods or services for cash only. If such a client is not willing or able to pay, simply cut off the deadbeat. Do not take unnecessary risks with the hope that your sales records are enhanced.

Remember, you are forming a business that will sometimes force you to do things that are not pleasant. Collecting on bad accounts is not an enjoyable process. But by being stern when necessary, and lenient when the circumstances allow, bad debts can be minimized.

Exhibit 4-1

Taylor Supplies Ltd. Accounts Receivable Table							
Customer	Acconts Receivable Total $	0–30 days	31–45 days	46–60 days	61–90 days	91–120 days	120 +
Genetta Construction	4,000	3,920					
Lion Buildings	9,000		4,500		4,500		
Mike's Plastics	14,000	3,000	3,800	3,200	2,000		2,000
Dante Lumber	8,400		8,400				
ACE Specialty Products	1,200	1,200					
Zebra Homes	5,000						5,000
Total	41,600	8,120	16,700	3,200	6,500		7,000

By utilizing this table, the various ages of accounts receivables can quickly be seen, and appropriate action by Taylor Supplies Ltd. can be implemented. All invoices in the 0-30 days category should be considered to be collectable, as well as those in the 31-45 days range. Unfortunately, once accounts have reached sixty days, people often become lax in paying them and so they stretch their accounts payable for an even longer period of time. The longer an account is outstanding, the less likely the client will shell out. Accounts in the 61-90 days category require strict attention, and Taylor Supplies should be extremely aggressive in attempting to collect these accounts. With accounts of 91 days and above, Taylor must be even more troublesome, perhaps utilizing the services of a lawyer or collection agency. It is worthwhile to note that accounts over 60 days are probably only about 20 percent of your total invoices outstanding, but these accounts will require about 80 percent of your time to collect.

By examining each account in the table individually, all kinds of interesting aspects of Taylor's collectables can be highlighted.

Genetta Construction

Genetta's total receivables are $4,000 of which only $3,920 are registered in the 0-30 day bracket. The likely reason for this is that Genetta has until the 21st of the month to take a two percent discount, after which the full $4,000 will be demanded. The next time Taylor creates an accounts receivable table, the $3,920 will likely be $4,000 unless Generta has already paid.

Lion Buildings

The total account outstanding here is $9,000 divided into two time periods. The fact that Lion has purchases outstanding from two different times indicates that they are probably a regular customer who attempts to stretch accounts payable. Taylor Supplies Ltd. must make certain that they are not too liberal with this firm, and that they receive payments soon. When these payments have not been received for over sixty days, it can be much more difficult to collect on this account.

Mike's Plastics

Mike's has been a regular shopper at the Taylor place and has built up the largest receivable totals. Mike's is probably a larger organization that has learned to take advantage of the largess of suppliers, extending accounts payable as fully as possible. It can be a dangerous practice to allow these clients to extend their credit too far, as eventually they consider longer payment terms to be policy, and this can have a severe negative impact on your cash flow situation.

Dante Lumber

Dante Lumber is probably stretching their accounts payable, perhaps to a 60-day limit. As they have bought a substantial amount at one time, it is likely that they are one of Taylor's older customers, and they have probably built up a credit record.

Ace Specialty Products

This is either a new account or a customer who appears to pay quickly. Taylor Supplies Ltd. can probably wait for payment in this instance; a payment will probably be forthcoming soon.

Zebra Homes

This account of over 120 days is above and beyond the danger zone. It is to be hoped Taylor has pressed them aggressively for payment, and perhaps a lawyer or collection agency has been employed. The likelihood of this account being written off as a bad debt is great. It would be interesting to know the relations between the two businesses and how this receivable of such a long duration occurred.

INVENTORY

For a retail business, inventory means the goods in the storerooms and on display for sale to customers. For a manufacturer, inventory consists of the raw materials used in production, the work-in-process, (i.e. cars on an assembly line), and the finished product for the consumer. Service firms rarely have an inventory, as inventory is only related to material goods.

Before the past recession, many firms had been living "fat," but with the onslaught of economic difficulties, "lean and mean" became a necessity. Realizing that efficient inventory control would save money, firms evaluated this area and implemented plans for a continuous inventory management system. The majority of these plans have remained in effect through better times.

A common estimate for the carrying cost of inventory is twice the prime rate — the prime rate being the borrowing rate granted a bank's best customers; therefore, if the prime rate is ten percent, inventory carrying costs are estimated at 20 percent. Some of these costs are as follows: additional storage space for the goods; cash used for inventory purchase that could be used more efficiently; obsolescence and deterioration; and employee time consumed to maintain the inventory.

The Ordering Point

When to order inventory presents a dilemma for many business people. A number of questions will help to clarify this "order point." These questions include: How much inventory is currently on hand? How quickly does the inventory usually sell? How much inventory must be on hand to satisfy customers' needs and avoid stock-outs? How long does supplier delivery take? What discounts are suppliers offering? How much money can the business currently spend on inventory?

To set this order point, many firms use one of three methods: "maximum-minimum control," "the open-to-buy method" and the "inventory total technique."

A) Maximum-Minimum Control

This technique establishes a maximum and minimum inventory level, above and below which inventory should never go. By estimating future sales and supplier time, orders are placed so that inventory will be replenished to the maximum level when the expected minimum inventory total is reached.

B) Open-to-Buy Method

This is a variation on the maximum-minimum control technique. Under this system, at any time inventory will be purchased so that the maximum level of stock is usually on hand. This technique can be vague as to when they order point is reached, sometimes causing stock-outs, or it can create consistently high inventory levels.

C) Inventory Total Technique

Using this technique, stock is reordered when the level reaches a pre-specified number. The amount ordered is enough to cover a future period, say four months. Sales estimation will also be necessary here.

When following any inventory buying method, it is important to recognize three key factors: the high cost of excess inventory; the loss of income because of stock-outs; and the advantage often presented by taking supplier's discounts. The inventory ordering technique should balance these three areas.

The Inventory Count

The inventory count helps to save money, reduce obsolescence and damage, and minimize theft. Three methods are commonly used.

The first method is a "visual control." Visual control simply means "eyeballing" and counting the inventory to make certain that everything is there. This technique is only appropriate for a small business, as a large operation has too much inventory for this to be feasible. To utilize this method, it is necessary that the merchandise be classified and differentiated to be recognized. Utilization of this system requires constant, regular monitoring; otherwise it cannot work.

A second method is a "physical count." This method differs from the visual control technique, as inventory is both counted and recorded; recording is not done with the visual control method. The physical count should be done at least *twice* a year, and often is handled by two people to help ensure accuracy. (See "Exhibit 4-2").

Exhibit 4-2

Physical Count Card			
Date	Item	Quantity Counted	Variance from Inventory Control
January 23	Hose	16	-1
	Tape	25	0
	Rope	18	0
	Hammers	14	-3
	Repair Kits	8	+1
	Bike Tires	12	0

The third method is "perpetual inventory control." Perpetual inventory control requires that every item be recorded when it arrives at the store, when it is stocked, and as it is sold. This process is very time-consuming, requiring a daily record to be logged, but a substantial benefit is that the inventory is always known; therefore, ordering points are easily identified. A computer can be useful here. (See "Exhibit 4-3").

Even if a perpetual inventory control system is in place, a physical count should be done also. This helps to account for all the inventory, noting loss from theft, breakage, or other damage.

Inventory Valuation

There are a number of different methods of valuing inventory. This will have an impact on the inventory valuation on the balance sheet, and also on the "cost of goods sold" section of the income statement. (See "The Income Statement" section). The greater the cost of goods sold, the lower will be the overall income, thus it will be necessary to pay less tax. For this reason, government is insistent that inventory be valued at the cost or the fair market value, whichever is lower, and that the valuation be consistent over time.

Valuation Method 1: FIFO

The most common method of valuing inventory in Canada is FIFO, which means; first in, first out. Using this system, the first inventory arriving is the first inventory sold. Though this might not necessarily be the case, it is considered to conform with the ordinary flow of inventory.

Example
A firm buys 42 units of inventory:

12 units in January for $3,000 each	= $36,000;
10 units in February for $3,500 each	= $35,000;
7 units in March for $3,500 each	= $24,500;
13 units in April for $3,700 each	= $48,100.
42 units bought for a total of	$143,600

Using FIFO, what is the inventory valuation if the firm sells 16 units?

Step 1
The inventory left is the 42 units minus the 16 units sold = 26 units.

Step 2
Since the last units would be the ones left in inventory, the first units would have been sold:

Exhibit 4-3

Perpetual Inventory Control Card
Hose

Reorder at 10 Units

Date	Supplier & Purchase #	Order Date	Delivery Date	Quantity Ordered	Quantity Received	Quantity Sold	# on Hand	Balance
Jan. 4	Tingle TRL5	Dec. 15	Jan. 4	10	10	3	8	15
5						2	15	13
6						1	13	12
12						4	12	8
13						2	8	6
15						3	6	3
16	Tingle TRL9	Jan. 12	Jan. 16	15	14	1	3	16
18						4	16	12

13 units purchased in April	= 48,100
7 units purchased in March	= 24,500
6 units purchased in Feb.	= 21,000
(6 x $3,500)	
26 units of inventory	= $93,600

Therefore the inventory valuation is $93,600.

Valuation Method 2: Lower-of-Cost-or-Market

This is another popular inventory valuation method. Using this technique, the stock is calculated at its cost or current market value, whichever is lower.

Using the example, what is the inventory valuation using the Lower-of-Cost-or-Market method if the firm sells 16 units?

Step 1
Once again, there would be 26 units left in inventory.

Step 2
To calculate the cost of the remaining inventory, invoices must be found for each item. In this case, let's assume the total value is $93,100.

Step 3
The "market" value is the current cost of buying the inventory. Assuming the cost of buying the inventory has remained the same as the April cost then:

26 units x $3,700
= $96,200

Therefore the inventory valuation is $96,200.

Step 4
Since $93,100 is less than $96,200, the $93,100 would be the inventory valuation.

Valuation Method 3: Weighted Average Cost

This method values the inventory on its average purchase price. Using the example gain, what is the inventory valuation using the Weighted Average Cost Method?

Step 1

Since it is unclear which units have been sold, the complete inventory must be used for our calculation.

Total Inventory ÷ Number of Units = Weighted Average Cost
$143,600 ÷ 42 = $3,419

Step 2

Since there are 26 units left in the inventory:

Weighted Average Cost x Units Remaining in Inventory = Inventory Valuation
$3,419 x 26 = $88,894
Valuation for inventory in this case is $88,894.

Valuation Method 4: LIFO

LIFO means: last in, first out; therefore the last inventory bought is the first inventory sold. This valuation method is no longer allowed in Canada as it increases the cost of goods sold substantially, reducing income and, therefore, tax payments. In addition to this, the method is somewhat unrealistic, as businesses could be claiming that their goods on hand were actually bought ten years ago, while the recently purchased inventory would all be sold. In countries where LIFO is allowed, it is extremely popular, especially during the inflationary times, when this method has the greatest impact.

Using the example, what is the inventory valuation using LIFO?

Step 1

Once again, there would be 26 units in inventory.

Step 2

Since the first units would be the ones left in inventory as the last units would have been sold:

12 units purchased in January	= $36,000
10 units purchased in February	= 35,000
4 units purchased in March	= 14,000
(4 x $3,500)	
26 units of inventory	= $85,000

Therefore the inventory valuation is $85,000.
What will the cost of goods sold be using LIFO and FIFO?

Using LIFO: Total Inventory - Inventory Remaining
=$143,600- $85,000
=$ 58,600

Using FIFO: Total Inventory - Inventory Remaining
= $143,600- $93,600
= $ 50,000

LIFO, therefore, would decrease earnings by $8,600, the difference between the two inventory valuations. This would reduce the tax rate, which is part of the reason the Canadian government does not allow this method.

Notice that in every case the various methods leads to a different inventory valuation; this will be reflected in a different value for the cost of goods sold. It is wise to choose the method that is most advantageous for your business, while remembering that the government is looking for consistency in approach, and is concerned that the valuation is at fair market value or cost, whichever is lower.

CHECKLIST 4-1 INVENTORY CONTROL CHECKLIST   YES   NO

Have customer needs and desires for products
     been analyzed?
Are goods being purchased consistent with
     the business image?
Is the seasonal business cycle being considered
     when ordering?
Are goods being analyzed and counted as they
     arrive at the store?

Are inventory counts being take regularly?
Are theft reduction methods in place?
Is the inventory correctly insured?
Are goods being stored in a manner
    to minimize damage?
Is the inventory space well-utilized?
Has an optimal order point been calculated?
Are stock-outs being avoided?
Has consideration been given to eliminate
    slow-moving inventory?
Is over-stocking being carefully watched?
Are supplier discounts being taken?
Are appropriate suppliers being utilized?

The more questions answered "Yes," the more efficiently your inventory is being managed.

Choosing Your Location

There is an old business adage that states, "There are three factors that make for a successful business: 'location, location, and location.'" Though certainly not the be-all and end-all of a small business, choosing the correct location is a key factor in the success or demise of an enterprise. The ideal site for the business will vary, depending on the type of enterprise.

The Manufacturing Location

Zoning laws usually restrict a manufacturing operation to certain industrial areas. When choosing one of these zones, it is important that the manufacturer consider the source for raw materials and the location of the marketplace.

Ideally, the manufacturer wants to be close to the source of raw materials. This becomes critical if the business is dealing with a perishable product, such as fruit, where time is of the essence to avoid spoilage. Being near raw materials is also important if the manufacturing process leads to large amounts of waste, because transportation costs can be greatly reduced, due to the reduction in weight.

Close access to the marketplace is also important. If it is possible, the firm should be situated near the centre of the client base, with a good transportation network to reach the consumer. Ultimately, the choice of location is usually a trade-off between access to raw materials and the marketplace.

There are a number of other considerations for the manufacturing firm when choosing a location. Some factors include: an adequate labour force; land for future expansion; an ample supply of energy; the rate of local taxation; and the possibility of government aid.

The Retail Location

Retailers have a number of areas to examine when selecting their location. Some of these considerations include surrounding businesses; traffic density; parking and transportation facilities; the competitors' locations; and the changing nature of the population.

It is important to locate in an area that is amenable to your specific clientele. For example: a "high society" boutique should not locate in the pawnbroker section of the city. The ideal location for this type of business would be in a trendy, fashion-conscious district, or perhaps a glittering shopping mall.

Traffic density is an important consideration. Some businesses, such as specialty shops, do not need a high traffic density to be successful, as customers will go out of their way to find the operation. But certain businesses need a constant traffic flow that is attracted into the store by fancy windows or an interesting sign. Without this flow, success is often impossible. To ensure this ongoing traffic, an adequate transportation network to reach the store, accompanied by parking facilities, is usually a necessity. A location without easy access is virtually useless.

Competitors' locations are important. Certainly a small furniture operator would not want to locate between The Brick and Leon's. But if the business is of sufficient size, it can be a good strategy to locate with the competition, setting up a "furniture alley," so that customers will be attracted to the area. Ultimately, this will increase the traffic flow of the target market.

The changing nature of the population is a factor in the site selection. Cities and towns change as population shifts to different neighbourhoods, as a seedy area is rejuvenated, as a once-posh area decays. Future population movements will be affected as industry thrives or dies, and you should be analyzing these possibilities, and forecasting how this will have an impact on your location and customer base.

Some other considerations include: the adequacy of the site for both the short- and long-term: the time it will take to travel to and from work every day; the lease that must be signed; and the nature of your landlord.

The Wholesale Location

Wholesalers in most cities are restricted by zoning laws. Within these area restrictions, it is usually critical that wholesalers can ensure their goods will reach the consumer quickly, as fast service is a key success variable for this type of business. To ensure prompt service, it is imperative that dealers locate dose to their clientele and have an efficient transportation network for their goods.

The Service Location

Locating the service firm depends on the type of consumer, the traffic flow necessary, and the image of the business. A travel agent's office must be fairly accessible, perhaps in a shopping mall, a repair shop can be more distant and isolated; an office selling theatre tickets might actually be a dingy corner room with a telephone. The key is providing customers with access to the sales people and not compromising the image of the business.

CHECKLIST 4-2

LOCATION CHECKLIST   YES   NO
Is the area currently suitable for your enterprise?
If the area is changing, are the changes positive
    for your business?
Is there a steady flow of traffic by the business site?
Does your target market shop in the area?
Is the customer base sufficient to support the venture?
Are neighbouring enterprises compatible with yours?

Are neighbouring enterprises doing well?
Are you appropriately situated in relation
    to the competition?
Is the location easily accessible to transportation?
Are there suitable parking facilities?
Can you comply with the zoning requirements?
Is the lease appropriate?
Does the landlord seem reasonable?
Is the tax rate appropriate?
Are there potential sources of government funding?
Are energy supplies sufficient?
Is there access to the necessary labour market?
Do suppliers have access to you?
Is the facility compatible with the firm's image?
Is the facility compatible with the business set-up?
Is there room for the enterprise to expand if
    this is desirable?
Have you carefully checked and compared other
    locations?

The more question answered "Yes," the better the choice of location.

WHERE TO SET UP: HOME VERSUS OFFICE DILEMMA

One question that immediately faces many new business people is whether to operate the venture from their home or set up an office. For some individuals, the answer to this question is quite simple, as the nature of their business dictates that working from the home is impossible. But for other aspiring entrepreneurs, the answer is not so clear-cut, and an evaluation of the pros and cons of home versus office is worthwhile.

Advantages of Working from the Home

1. Working from the house or apartment can reduce costs dramatically. Some of these costs include:

A) Travel Costs

$0.00. Instead of spending money on operating your car or riding on public transit, you simply stay home and begin working. This can easily save hundreds of dollars annually.

B) Rental Costs

$0.00. To rent an office space costs a substantial amount of money. By establishing an office at home, you can actually receive a tax deduction from the government. (See "Minimize Those Taxes" section). Rent is a major expenditure of thousands of dollars that, if avoided, can provide working capital for the operation, or simply allow for the monetary saving that might make the venture feasible.

C) Insurance and Hydro Costs

$ Minimal. Insurance, hydro, and other expenses, such as an additional telephone, can be reduced or eliminated. Once again, large amounts of capital will be saved.

D) Lunch Costs

$ Minimal. Though often not considered by the office-bound, lunches are one of those expenses that quickly add up. Rather than going to the office and buying lunch three or four or five times a week, just head to the refrigerator and make yourself a meal. If this habit saves you $30 a week on average, $1,500 annually is not consumed by lunch money.

E) Clothing Cost

$ Minimal. Working at home allows for a minimal wardrobe. Certainly, when meeting a client, dressing for success is important, but working from the home makes it simpler to schedule appointments so that you can avoid office dress every day of the week. This also increases convenience and helps avoid the aggravation of contemplating daily, "What should I wear today?"

F) Staff Cost

$0.00. With an office, a person is often needed to maintain the premises while the boss is gone. By working from home, this cost is eliminated.

2. Working from the home also has some advantages that are not of a monetary nature. These advantages include:

A) Travel Time

On average, it takes a person between one and two hours per day travelling to and from work. Working from the home allows this time to be spent beneficially, as time that would be spent in transit can be utilized doing business work.

B) Flexibility and Convenience

Working from the home allows you to arrange your working day at your convenience. If a brilliant idea is conceived and you need your notes right away for verification, you do not have to race to the office to retrieve them, but simply walk to the appropriate room and begin to work. This flexibility and convenience allows for greater efficiency and saves copious amounts of time.

Disadvantages of Working from the Home

Working from the home also has a number of disadvantages, otherwise almost everyone would do it. Some of these disadvantages include:

A) Lack of Privacy

Often family and friends assume that because you work from the house, they can bother you at their leisure since, "You're probably not really working anyhow." This might be fine for the social life, but odds are that it will hinder the business life. It is critical, therefore, to make people realize that you do keep office hours, and that working during those hours is essential.

B) Distractions

Soap operas, telephone conversations, chores that "must" be done, like straightening the magazines twelve times a day (you keep reading them, therefore they must need straightening), and a host of other distractions can easily lead you to do anything but work. Distractions are a major drawback when attempting to work from the home. I have heard more stories from well-intentioned individuals who simply cannot quite "get down to it" and have been forced to abandon their venture.

The key here is discipline. Working from the home is rarely possible for an individual who does not have a strong sense of discipline. Without it, odds are that the business will quickly fail.

C) Lack of Visibility

By-laws and the neighbours often make it difficult to have the visibility that might be desired for the operation. Even though you are a wonderful person, your neighbours do not wish to have a sign eighteen feet by twenty-four feet hanging from the apartment building, advertising your superior wares. This can create difficulties, as you try to make the public cognisant of the enterprise.

D) Image

Sometimes it is very difficult to project the ideal business image to the public when working from the home. For this reason, an office might be a necessity.

E) Inability to Leave the Work Place

Many people find that it is necessary for their sanity to have one place to work and another to live. By combining home and office, they feel uncomfortable, as work becomes omnipresent, therefore making it impossible for them to have a reprieve. Other individuals who combine home and office have a tendency to work all the time, constantly attracted by the apparent need to do more and more for their business. Often this becomes self-defeating, as they begin to stagnate, or major social difficulties are created as they ignore family and friends. Distancing oneself from the office becomes the solution, and is a logical necessity for many individuals.

F) Moulding the Business to the Home

When an individual searches for an office, he tries to find a location that is suitable for the needs of the business. But the individual who works from the home, usually has a prescribed space to work from and, therefore, moulds the business to that space. This can prove ineffective for the needs of the business.

Statistically, a far higher percentage of businesses succeed when operated from the home rather than the office. Primarily, this is because for most new businesses, capital is extremely limited, and operating from the house can save thousands upon thousands of dollars. An excellent plan of attack for many new ventures is to commence operations from the home and, if successful, to open an office when the cash flow and profitability situation allow. In this way, the market can be tested, clientele established, and many of the kinks eliminated from the operation, before the greater office expenses are incurred.

When considering the home versus office question, think carefully about the business you are establishing. Many services, mail order operations, and light distribution or wholesale enterprises, are extremely successful operating from the home. Their common ingredients are that they all have limited inventory, need few employees, and will not offend the neighbours.

Exhibit 4-4

Home versus Office	
Home Advantages	**Office Advantages**

1. Cost Related:
   A) Travel
   B) Rent
   C) Insurance and Hydro
   D) Lunches
   E) Clothes
   F) Staff
   G) Taxes
 	
2. Not Cost Related:
   A) Travel Time Saved
   B) Flexibility and Convenience
	A) Greater Privacy
	B) Fewer Distractions
	C) Greater Visibility
	D) Enhanced Image
	E) Separation of Office and Home
	F) Choice of Space

LAYOUT

Layout is the manner in which the space of the business is set up. The type of business: retail, wholesale, manufacturer, or service, has a major impact on the optimal layout arrangement. Within each of these business types, specific layout rules must be considered.

The Retail Layout

The "utilization of space" concept is of prime importance for the retail layout: maximize the usage of space, while enhancing the image of the business. A bargain-basement clothing store might have tables with pants strewn every which way, while a posh fashion clothier will have everything meticulously arranged, so that both the items and the customers have their own display space.

Items of a similar type should be merchandised together, which provides convenience for the consumer and when shelving the products. For example: toiletries would be grouped together in one section with pharmaceuticals in another area.

Certain activities in the store should also be separated. Usually the selling areas should be distinct from non-selling activities, such as the service department, repair shop, or accounting section.

The store layout should also take advantage of lighting, ventilation, and heat. Used correctly, lighting can enhance the colours of certain products, making them more attractive, and increasing the likelihood of a sale. Proper ventilation and a correct thermostat setting will help to encourage customers to stay in the store, increasing the chances that they will purchase something.

Understanding consumer buying habits will also aid in the store set-up. Because the majority of customers tend to look to their right as they enter a store, it is beneficial to have high mark-up items to the right. By placing necessities at the back of the location, customers will be induced to venture through the store, passing by numerous other items. This can help create the possibility of the purchase of a "non-essential" or "impulse" item. But the front area remains the prime selling space, as most customers do not walk to the back of the shop, unless necessary.

Another consideration when designing the layout is shoplifting. This is unfortunate, but necessary, as these incidents have been increasing in regularity in recent years. Many businesses have been attempting to cope by placing metallic tags on goods, that must be removed by salespeople, or a buzzer will sound if someone attempts to leave the store with an item without paying. For businesses that cannot afford this type of system, strategically-placed mirrors can be an excellent aid. Creating dear sight lines from the cash area to the easily pocketed items can also be useful in reducing theft. Lastly, a simple, "May I help you?" as the customer enters the store is often enough to discourage shoplifters.

The optimal layout for a retail outlet takes into account the normal space valuation for each area in the store. The following exhibit helps to demonstrate this.

Table 4-1

Space Valuation		
Lowest Space Valuation	Seventh Highest Space Valuation	Lowest Space Valuation
Sixth Highest Space Valuation	Fifth Highest Space Valuation	Second Highest Space Valuation
Fourth Highest Space Valuation	Second Highest Space Valuation	Highest Space Valuation
WINDOW	DOOR	WINDOW

The Wholesale Layout

Wholesalers must concentrate on developing a different layout arrangement from retailers, a key consideration being that over 60 percent of a wholesalers' costs are usually consumed by labour. For this reason, it is crucial that the layout be designed so that the product can be received, stored, and shipped easily. To do this, high volume products must be easily accessible. Specialized equipment can be useful here, and also help to maximize the potential storage area.

The Manufacturing Layout

Manufacturing layout must minimize wasted movement that does not add value to the product. An example of this is inventory that must constantly be moved when new shipments arrive. Value is not added to the product, but costs are created by the labour necessary. For this reason, raw materials should be received near the point where they will be utilized. Finished goods should be completed near the location where they will be stored and/or shipped to the market.

For the single-product factory, designing a space in which wasted movement is limited is much easier to accomplish than for an operation that produces multiple products. In either situation, it is wise to study a number of potential layouts, if possible before the facility is built, and certainly before equipment is installed. This can reduce problems substantially and save tremendous amounts of money.

The Service Layout

Services vary dramatically in nature, and they have few binding rules for layout. However, when designing their layout, three characteristics should be considered. First, image is important. A shoe repair shop can be cluttered and dirty looking, but this will rarely discourage customers, while a hairdressing salon must have a nice reception area and hospitable surroundings. Second, the layout must satisfy the customers' needs. In the shoe repair store, customers need limited space, while in the hair salon, much more room is required for every client. The last consideration is the volume of business. Many services have few customers but large sales and, therefore, need minimum space for their clientele. Other services have a small number of individual sales, but a large number of total sales, and so require more space.

By planning and implementing the optimal layout for your business, sales can be increased and costs can be reduced. This will add to the profitability of your business.

MARKETING

Marketing is "Getting the right product to the right people at the right price, the right time, and the right place."

In this definition, the "Four P's" of marketing: Price, Promotion, Place, and Product become more apparent. This is known as the marketing mix. The analysis of each component of the marketing mix will aid in the creation of a marketing plan with dear goals and objectives.

The Price Component

The first "P," price, will have a major effect on the sales of the product or service. One factor to consider is the "price elasticity." Price elasticity refers to the change in quantity of a product consumed, relative to the change in the price of the product. For example: if the price of a Jaguar is $40,000, and consideration is being given to raising the price by 50 percent to $60,000, what quantity would be consumed? By knowing the price elasticity for Jaguars, the resulting sales can be estimated, and this would indicate whether the price raise would be worthwhile. If demand decreased by only 10 percent, then profits should skyrocket. Knowledge of the price elasticity of a product or service allows you to set the price so that profit is maximized.

Price elasticity is dependent on whether the product is a necessity or a luxury: for necessities, a change in price will not lead to a substantial change in sales volume, as these goods must be purchased anyway; luxuries, on the other hand, are more responsive to price changes.

Keeping price elasticity in mind, the following are methods for pricing:

A) Cost Pricing

Cost pricing is a simple and popular method of valuing products. This method takes the cost of the product and adds on a percentage. If a cassette costs the store $2 and the standard mark-up is 100 percent of the cost, then the cassette will retail for $4. Furniture outlets, grocery stores, booksellers, and numerous other industries use this method.

B) Target Pricing

Target pricing is setting the price of an item so that a desired rate of return will be achieved. The first step in target pricing is to calculate costs and decide on a desired rate of return; then sales must be estimated. For example: A man enters the sporting goods industry, specializing in ski packages. He expects to sell 100 ski packages and his total costs will be $20,000. He desires a rate of return of 10 percent on his costs. What would his target price be for each package?

To achieve a 10 percent return on $20,000, sales must be $22,000. If 100 packages are to be sold, then each package must sell for $220 to achieve this return.

Notice that this technique relies heavily on sales estimation. This can present a problem if sales are not estimated accurately.

C) Demand Oriented Pricing

Demand oriented pricing is set on the perceived value of the product or service. The greater the demand, the higher the price; the lower the demand, the lower the price. In certain instances, this can lead to outrageous prices. The stock market is influenced by demand oriented pricing, as prices are set in many instances on perception of worth, rather than real value, creating overvalued and undervalued situations.

D) Competition Oriented Pricing

In this situation, prices are set in relation to the competition. Sometimes the prices are identical, but at other times the strategy is to set prices higher or lower, based on location, image, or other factors. Often, the more intensified the level of competition, the closer the prices will be.

All of these pricing strategies are perfectly valid and may be applied to various business situations. Many businesses use a combination of these methods, in determining the price for their products. Whichever method you choose, it is still necessary to be aware of your costs, the demand for the product or service, and the price being charged by the competition.

The Promotion Component

Promotion is comprised of four areas: sales promotion; advertising; personal selling and publicity.

Sales promotion refers to events to lure customers to your products. It includes areas such as discount coupons, two-for-one specials, tag days, and other specials. Some operators employ this technique on a daily basis, while other business people choose to be more selective, having a boxing day sale or a spring sale. This will depend on the image you want to present. When choosing to have a sales promotion, the costs of the promotion must be compared with the revenues.

An advertisement is a public announcement, usually used to persuade someone to do something. One of the major decisions in the advertising area is the medium chosen for the business. Some selections include radio, television, newspapers, and various magazines. The decision on which media form is best will depend largely on the promotional budget and optimal method to reach the target market. (See "Who Will Your Customers Be" section).

Personal selling is the work of both the owner and the salespeople. A good salesperson can increase sales dramatically by encouraging clientele to purchase larger quantities (i.e. suggestive selling: "Do you need a tie to go with that suit?"), by arranging exhibits neatly, and by being innovative in the selling approach.

Last is the publicity component. Publicity refers to promotion obtained free. This can fit into all business people's budgets. For the innovative owner, a wealth of sales can be generated this way. Newspapers, radio stations, and television programmes are often "starved" for information and are looking for anything "newsworthy." Some ideas to make your business newsworthy include, creating a story for your local newspaper when you commence operations; renting a camel and placing it in front of the store, then having a friend phone the news and say, "Hey! There's a camel in front of this guy's store!"; becoming an expert guest on topics relating to your industry and speaking on radio or television shows; informing the media of community work that your business is doing. A creative mind can generate fantastic amounts of media coverage. This can have a dramatic impact on sales and provide some fun.

The Place Component

"Place" refers to the process of distributing the product to the market, and the final selling location which is dependent on the target market. The two primary questions in the place component of the marketing mix, therefore, are: What form of distribution will be used for the product to reach the market? and which consumers will the product be targeted for?

In most distribution decisions, there are numerous channel choices. For example: when an envelope must reach Ottawa from Toronto, a decision must be made as to the optimal channel of distribution. Canada Post is one channel that will take a few days but at a very low cost. A courier service which is quicker, is another channel option, but this will be more expensive. Lastly, you might consider driving to Ottawa yourself so that the letter will reach its destination that very afternoon. Of course, this would be even more expensive and take a tremendous effort on your part, but it does present a channel option. The primary trade-off between these three channels of distribution, as with most channel decisions, is the cost of reaching the destination versus the time involved.

The more channels of distribution that a product encounters on its way from the manufacturer to the market, the more levels the channel is considered to have. The shortest channel is a product that goes directly from the producer to the consumer. This is a two level channel, as two groups are in contact with the product. In most cases, a product will go from the producer to a retailer to the consumer. This is a three level channel. Some channels of distribution have upwards of ten channels to pass through.

Choosing the optimal network of channels is of prime strategic importance. This can reduce costs, guarantee serving the consumer efficiently, make certain that the target market is reached, and therefore, ultimately, enhance profits. A small businessperson however, will often be restricted in the choice of channels of distribution, therefore curtailing where the product can be sold. Some reasons for the channel limitation include middle people who will not handle an unproven businessperson's products; limited business resources and, therefore, a lack of funds to buy the best channel; and competitors who are fully utilizing existing channels.

To decide on the optimal channel of distribution, first select the target market that is desired. Once this market is outlined, then evaluate the cost and time efficiencies of having your product reach the marketplace. In almost every case, the more quickly the channel allows the product to reach the market, the more expensive the distribution method; therefore, a decision must be made on the optimal time for the product to reach the market. Often careful planning will allow a slower mode of distribution at a reduced cost, while still serving the consumer effectively.

The Product Component

When considering this component of the marketing mix, various aspects of the product should be carefully analysed. The desired quality of the product should be outlined; a strategy might be adopted to produce a premium quality good and sell it for a premium price, or perhaps a lower quality product will be produced, hoping to attract a larger marketplace. Different product features must also be considered; usually the more features, the higher the price. Packaging can have a major impact on how the product sells with size, shape, and colour being key variables. The service level and warranty associated are also important considerations. The better the service and warranty guarantees, the higher the associated costs. An in-depth analysis of the various aspects of the product or service is a must.

Different strategic decisions are made, regarding the marketing mix that will determine the "positioning" for the product or service in the marketplace. For example: producing a premium quality product and selling it for a high price is called a "premium" strategy. This strategy will likely lead to sales in fairly select outlets, where status or quality concerns might be critical for the consumer. At the other end of the spectrum would be a low quality low priced item. This is considered to be a "cheapy" strategy, and a product such as this would probably have a limited guarantee, if any. The following chart indicates some of the price-product trade-offs and the accompanying marketing strategy. Remember that the choice of any of these options will affect the place where the goods are sold, the channels of distribution, the promotional method, and the firm's goals and objectives.

It is also important to consider that once a reputation is established, it can be difficult to change. When considering the optimal marketing mix for your enterprise, therefore, it is important to ponder both short- and long-term considerations.

Chart 4- 1

Marketing Mix Strategies				
		High	**Price** **Medium**	**Low**
	Low	Fast Buck* Strategy	Overpricing Strategy	Cheapy Strategy
Product Quality	Medium	Overpricing Strategy	Fair Market Value Strategy	Good Deal Strategy
	High	Premium Strategy	Penetration** Strategy	Super Bargain Strategy

Footnotes for chart:

*Fast Buck Strategy — people will usually not be fooled by an inferior product twice, so entrepreneurs who choose this method often make quick dollars, and then look for another line of work.

**Penetration Strategy — trying to make fast inroads into a marketplace by having an undervalued price for a product. Designed to undercut competition and grab a greater market share; market share is the percentage of the overall market that buys from a business (also can be applied to specific products or services).

WHAT'S IN A NAME?

The name you choose for your business can greatly improve your chances for success. Ideally, the name should convey an image that indicates to prospective customers the business that you are in, and how you can help them to fulfil their needs. The easiest method to do this is to select a name that mentions the nature of the business that you are establishing. For example: Plumbing Suppliers, The Lumber Place, The Hardware Shop, and Mr. Shoe Repair are all instantly identified with specific enterprises.

Many firms choose to personalize their business name, an aspect

Exhibit 4-5

Interaction of the Four P's

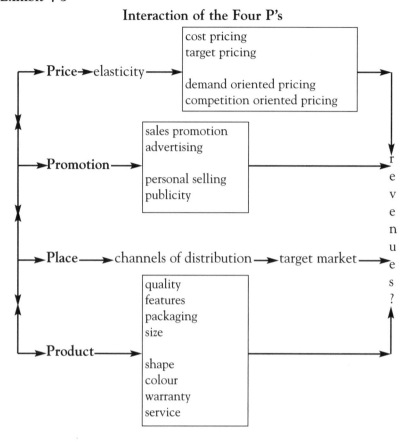

that appeals to customers who are searching for prompt, efficient, personal service. Examples of this are: Russell's Variety, Bill's Sporting Goods, and Elizabeth Ame's Clothing For Women. This technique can also serve as a useful marketing tool, for when Elizabeth Ame makes personal appearances, she will actually be promoting both herself and the business.

Many ventures choose a name that evokes an image of specific characters. Common tides in this case include: Grandma's, Lil Bobby's, or Rascals. The important ingredient here is that the name fits the likeness of the business.

Unless you are operating the business under your own name, make certain that a "name search" is done for your operation. This is very inexpensive. Many businesses have opened, and after spending thousands of dollars on signs, business cards, and promotions, have found that they are using an established business name. The consequences can be a nasty lawsuit and/or the necessity to change to another name. Both consume money and time.

Another technique to establish the business is a logo. For provincial or national firms, a logo can be worthwhile as a promotional tool; but for the small, local operation, a logo usually has an extremely limited identification value. It is more valuable for the small business to utilize its limited capital resources in a more efficient manner.

Before finalizing your business name, "run it by" family and friends. See if they think the title sounds good. Sometimes, an owner picks a name without any research and this can lead to a shoddy selection. By obtaining other people's opinions, a name should be chosen that identifies and describes your business. This will boost sales and profits.

WHO WILL YOUR CUSTOMERS BE?

Defining your customers is an important part of the marketing strategy. The more dearly that your clientele is identified, the easier it is to advertise correctly, to act upon customer's wants and needs, and, ultimately, to increase sales.

In some instances, it is fairly easy to state who the customers for a business will be. For example: an expensive dress shop will depend on clientele who are female of the upper and middle class. A video arcade attracts mostly males between the ages of sixteen and thirty-five. A store specializing in baseball cards will attract males between the ages of ten and twenty-five. For some businesses, however, the clientele mix is less clear, and the process of "market segmentation" becomes extremely useful.

Market segmentation is a process in which the population is divided into smaller components until those who are most likely to purchase a product or service are identified. Once this group is found, it becomes the "target market" — the market that should be concentrated upon to produce sales.

Market segmentation concentrates on the question of who the clientele for the business will be. But segmentation should lead you to ask additional questions, such as: Why do these people buy? What do they buy? When will they buy? Where do the customers come from? How are they likely to hear about the business? By answering these questions, a far clearer image of your clientele will emerge.

Once these questions are answered, the "key success variables" will become clearer. Key success variables are the major factors that will help you succeed in the business. Will people shop at your location because of price? Is service the crucial ingredient? Is it because your goods are extremely fresh? By identifying your key success variables, additional desires of your target market will be understood, and this will help you to identify and satisfy your marketplace more completely.

There are numerous methods of segmenting the marketplace. Three of these methods are: "Life Style Stages," "Personality Types," and "Product Specific Behaviour."

"Life style stages" divides the population into eight groups: the singles stage; newly married couples; full nest I, II, and III; empty nest I and II; and solitary survivors. Simply by the names, you should have a fairly good idea about the composition of each of these segments. The key, as you read through the information on each of these groups, is to be answering some of the aforementioned questions, as you identify the target market for your product or service.

Stage 1: Singles

Typically, this stage features young males and females whose earned income is low, but whose discretionary income — the income they can spend in any manner they choose — is high. This is because singles usually do not have to support a family, often live at home, and their spending on necessities is, therefore, limited. Generally, people in this category spend a tremendous amount of their earnings on vacations; recreation; fashion; kitchen equipment; and — that oldest of pastimes — the mating game.

Stage 2: Newly Married Couples

At this juncture is a young couple, probably working. Financially, they are in a better position as a couple than they were previously as singles, as expenses can be shared. This segment has the highest average purchase rate for durable goods of any group. Newly-marrieds tend to spend a lot of money on cars, clothing, and vacations.

Stage 3: Full Nest I

Congratulations! The baby has arrived! But among all of the joys, there are indeed a number of hardships. The wife sometimes stops working, meaning a loss of income for the family. Space becomes more limited as the baby demands room. In addition to this, furniture must be bought for the little one, and there are all kinds of other financial demands to meet baby's needs. This group is the most dissatisfied with their financial position, and tend to stay home more which helps save money.

In this stage, the couple is most susceptible to advertising and new products. There are three major reasons for this. First, because they stay home so much, they generally watch more television. This means they see more advertisements. Second, the couple is starting to buy many new products with which they are not experienced, therefore, they watch the advertisements more carefully. Third, they have a tendency to hunt for bargains, be it through newspapers, radio ads, or when watching television, as another evening is passed with baby.

Stage 4: Full Nest II

At this stage, the financial situation tends to improve. Though there might be more children, there is additional income as the husband moves up the income scale at the office, while the wife returns to the work force. Both are less influenced by advertisements as they have more buying experience. Money tends to be spent on food; cleaning materials; bicycles; musical instruments; and various lessons for the children.

Stage 5: Full Nest III

At this point, family finances improve again, as the husband, usually the wife, and maybe even the children, are working. Expenses increase as the family replaces older items with new ones, generally buying goods that are considered to be more tasteful. A large portion of the family's income is spent on travel, cars, dental bills, and magazines.

Stage 6: Empty Nest I

Yes, the children have left, and with their departure, the couple's financial position is the best it has ever been. Husband and wife are at their optimal earning power and they tend to spend their money on travel, recreation, self-education, gifts, and luxuries.

Stage 7: Empty Nest II

At this point, there is a reduction in income as one, or perhaps both, of the spouses leave their employment. There is a tendency to stay home more. Additional funds are spent on medical needs, especially health, sleep, and digestion.

Stage 8: Solitary Survivors

At this stage, one spouse dies. There is the possibility that the home is then sold. If the survivor continues to work, a large portion of the income is used for vacations or health, but when the widow or widower is not working, there can be a drastic drop in income, which may severely curtail a diverse lifestyle. In either of these cases, the survivor desires affection and attention, and has numerous anxieties about security.

By analysing these lifestyles stages, you should be able to perceive the target market for your product or service. In some cases, this method may only partially help to define your market, and you should continue to define your target market more clearly. Another segmentation technique based on personality types might be useful here.

Personality segmentation helps to identify the key characteristics and interests of the clientele. By knowing this, you can make the necessary decisions that will attract customers to your product or service.

For example: Bob is a 32-year-old construction worker who watches a tremendous amount of sports, drinks a case of beer a week, and enjoys little more than spending his evenings at home and weekends fishing. Bob might represent 12 percent of the male population.

Jim, on the other hand, is a stockbroker who prides himself on his dress, goes dancing three times a week, and loves to take vacations to exotic resorts. Jim might represent nine percent of the male population.

These two gentlemen will purchase vastly different products and services. Will your customers be Bobs or Jims?

Product specific behaviour is a third segmentation technique that is often utilized. This type of segmentation is intended to measure the behaviour or attitude of individuals toward a product or service. The most important element of product specific behaviour is the usage rate of the consumer. By discovering which consumer group is a heavy, medium, or light user of the product, a marketing programme can be designed to appeal to the major clients and also encourage medium and lighter users to increase their purchases.

Product specific behaviour can also help to define the consumer's loyalty towards a specific product, brand, or organization. It can identify whether consumers tend to buy products when they first appear on the shelves, or wait until their neighbours try them and give them approval. By utilizing this information effectively, a clearer perception of your customer will be obtained, which will help you to form strategies to attract your target market. Ultimately, this will increase your sales.

PREPARING A MARKETING PLAN

Preparing a marketing plan takes a good deal of work. Many people consider the plan to be simply choosing the media and then advertising. But a well-designed marketing plan goes far beyond that. The following steps will help in the plan's design.

Step 1: State Your Marketing Goals and Objectives

The marketing goals and objectives must be compatible with both your business and personal goals and objectives. If you want the business to be an industry leader in the retail sector, odds are that a substantial marketing budget will be necessary, and you must be willing and able to spend this money on advertising. The marketing goals and objectives should state dearly that the desire is to claim industry leadership, and for this a substantial marketing budget will be necessary. This will give focus to the plan.

Step 2: Outline Your Image

The image portrayed to the public by the business will have a major impact on the number and the type of your clientele. You should make certain that the image the business portrays is compatible with the location and yourself.

Step 3: Decide On the Key Selling Features

Why is it that customers will consume your products or services? Is it a good location, a low pricing strategy, or perhaps your personal charisma? When you identify your key selling features, choosing a marketing strategy becomes easier.

Step 4: Check Your Products

Are your products compatible with your image? If the business is expected to survive, and the plan is to charge consumers premium prices, then ill-made products will not be good enough.

Step 5: Decide on a Pricing Strategy

Your pricing strategy is usually a key component of your key selling features; although in some instances, it is not of prime importance. Still, in either case, the pricing strategy must be recognized and implemented as a marketing tool. This strategy will evaluate costs, market demand, the competition's pricing policy and the elasticity of pricing.

Step 6: Analyse Why Customers Buy Your Product

If the business is the sale of fur coats, then prestige will likely be a major factor for customers; for the Goodwill organization, customers will shop because of price; if you wish to sell underarm deodorant, fear is a factor in the customer's purchasing decision. Understanding the purchasing rationale is an aid in your marketing campaign.

Step 7: Set Out a Customer Profile

Define your customer as completely as possible. Market segmentation will be useful here. The more characteristics that can be used to define the consumer, the more exact the promotional plan will be.

Step 8: Define the Selling Place

If the business is a single retail outlet, the location choice can be difficult, but once chosen, the selling place is set. For a small producer or middleman, who might be distributing to a number of locations, a continuous evaluation of the channels of distribution and the final selling location must be constantly analysed.

Step 9: Develop a Marketing Budget

The marketing budget is a part of the cash flow projection. (See "Planning Your Cash Flow" section). Within this budget, make certain that an adequate amount of funding is allocated to the marketing section, so that the marketing goals and objectives are feasible. Naturally, this budget must be created remembering that the business is limited in its resources and that only so many dollars can be allocated to the marketing domain.

Step 10: State the Strengths and Weaknesses of Your Business

Promotion should be done from strength. The discovery of weaknesses should lead to an attempted correction of those difficulties.

Step 11: Review and Choose An Appropriate Promotional Method

What method will be best to reach your target market at the lowest price? This is the key question here. Perhaps it will be television, newspapers, magazines, or radio. Maybe the marketing budget cannot afford these areas, and you will be forced to rely strictly on free publicity, business cards, flyers, and word-of-mouth sales.

Step 12: Create the Advertising and Make Certain That It Fits Your Image

Step 12 returns us to step number 2. Advertisements must be created with the business's image in mind, and the customers' needs must be considered. It is wise, therefore, that before advertising, you have family, friends, or advisers check to make sure that the ads actually say what you think they say — that they promote the business in an appropriate manner. This will help to attract your target market.

Step 13: Implement the Plan

Once everything has been checked and double-checked to make certain that all appears reasonable and logical and compatible with your goals and objectives, then implement the plan. Remember though, that this is an ongoing process, and as the business develops and changes, a re-analysis of each of these steps should be undertaken. Updating will help to ensure that the business remains current, and that it satisfies both continuous and changing market needs.

CASE 5: JOAN'S STUFFED DOLLS

Joan Dewie was baffled. She had been working as a legal secretary for eight years and was becoming bored with the job. She realized though, that a second income was a necessity, as she and her husband Don had just purchased a house and assumed a large mortgage. It would be impossible to cover payments on his salary alone.

Recently, Joan had been asked by about half a dozen of her friends and co-workers to make her "Dolly" dolls as Christmas presents for their children. Joan had been making Dolly dolls sporadically for about three years. She had produced an average of two a month, with each doll taking about eight hours to make. The majority of the labour consisted of the stitching, about which Joan was meticulous, taking pride in her ability to make a doll that would withstand the punishment of the most "beastly" of children. Joan used only quality wool and cotton in her dolls, and sold each for $10, which equalled her costs. She never charged for her services, considering the work a hobby, and happy that others would find delight in her craft.

One Saturday afternoon, Joan and Don were wandering around the exclusive shopping district of Toronto's Yorkville. She noticed that one store sold dolls that were similar to hers for $110. "That's a ludicrous price!" Joan cried. "I can't believe that they charge that much! The stitching is not even very good!"

From Yorkville, Don and Joan went on an exploratory mission throughout the city, and found that dolls were far more expensive than either could have imagined.

"You know Don," Joan began, as they returned home, "Maybe I should start my own doll-making business. But I wouldn't have a clue whether to work from home or set up a store. I know that I could keep working as a legal secretary part-time. Maybe I should do it?"

What should Joan do?

CASE 6: THE JONSON SAGA: PART I

Dave and Dolly Jonson were watching reruns of "Dallas" on the VCR when Dolly shouted, "We can do it!" "Do what?" Dave said sleepily. "We can start the catering service." "Oh, that again," Dave said.

"I just want to do some market planning and, who knows, we could be as rich as the Ewings!"

"You've got to be kidding," said Dave.

"I rarely kid," stated Dolly flatly, which was true. "What I want to think of are the different aspects of the market that must be considered: 'Who, when, where, why, and how.'"

"'Who, when, where, why, and how' what?" Dave asked quizzically.

"Not what," Dolly stated. "I know what I will sell already. But who will the customers be? When will my big season be? Where will I cater? Why will people buy from me? And how am I going to promote the business?"

"You'll have to know that plus about a zillion other things," chirped Dave.

"I know, I know," confirmed Dolly. "But first I'll have fun with this. Then I'll think about other things another time. Besides, I can't sit here and watch re-runs of "Dallas" with you all the time! You must have seen this episode six times!"

"Seven. But it's a good one," stated Dave.

"I don't know," said Dolly, with a shake of her head. "Sometimes I wonder how you get by."

"Simple," said David. "I have really good peripheral vision."

"Oh David. That is really dumb."

"Thank you," he said to Dolly's back, as she departed the room.

What did Dolly's marketing outline look like?

PART V

How I Hate Those Numbers!

When I taught how to start a small business, most of the people in my classes had a tremendous desire to start their own business. Many of my students also had a tremendous fear of numbers. This is a problem when an individual wants to begin a venture.

Because of this difficulty faced by so many of my students, I tailored my teaching method so that just about everyone could understand the numerical aspects of starting and operating a business. This technique comprised teaching and preparing cases that give the students a chance to gain comprehension gradually. My teaching experience helped greatly in the creation of this book.

The majority of the following sections have various financial statements and calculations that should be understood by someone starting an enterprise. Most of the difficulties you will face can be overcome by application; but some individuals see numbers and simply say, "I can't do that," and, therefore, they don't. I taught hundreds of people, and can report that of those who have made a real effort, over 95 percent were able to understand the vast majority of the following sections.

Numerous books about starting a business completely ignore or gloss over the numerical aspects of the starting and operating situations. Though apparently kind to some readers, these books actually do the readers, who are seriously considering their own venture, a grave disservice. For those who attempt to start an operation without knowledge in the numerical area are ready to be claimed as business casualties.

Give the following section a good honest effort. You might not understand everything, but if the majority of the information is digested, you will have increased your chances for business success dramatically!

Profit or Loss? The Income Statement

The income statement is the financial information that indicates the profit or loss for the operation. As the "bottom line" for your business, this statement is of particular significance.

The income statement usually covers a period of one year. Sometimes, businesses choose to publish a statement that covers a shorter period of time: semi-annual or quarterly statements, but for most small ventures, annual statements should suffice.

At the top of the income statement is the name of the business. (See "Exhibit 5-1"), followed by "Income Statement" and the time period covered. After this, "Gross Sales" (1) appears on many income statements. This is the total of all the sales in the respective period, even those sales for which cash has not been received. Following gross sales is "Returns and Allowances" (2). This would allow for items that were returned because they were unsatisfactory, or an allowance made because a person was dissatisfied with the product, and therefore a discount was allowed. This leads to the "Net Sales" (3) category, which is derived from subtracting the returns and allowances from the gross sales.

The next category on the income statement is the "Cost of Goods Sold" (4). Cost of goods sold appears on the statement for non-manufacturing operations. To calculate the cost of goods sold is fairly simple; it is just the cost that the business pays for its product, including freight, duty, and other accompanying expenses. For example: if a business sold five stuffed teddy bears at $50 each, and the cost if each bear was $25, sales would be $250, and the cost of goods sold $125; then by subtracting the cost of goods sold from the net sales, the "Gross Profit" (5) is derived which, in this case, would be $125.

Operating expenses are the costs of running the business — appear next on the income statement. There are far too many of these to indicate in this chapter, but some of the most common expenses include: "Salaries" (6), "Rent" (7), "Promotion" (8), "Transport" (9), "Hydro" (10), "Depreciation" (11), and "Miscellaneous" (12). A common mistake for many novice entrepreneurs is to forget to include depreciation on the income statement. It is extremely important that you include all of your expenses. This will reduce your total income level and, consequently, your taxes.

"Total Expenses" (13), the sum of the operating expenses appears next on the income statement. By subtracting this from the gross profit, you have calculated your "Net Profit Before Tax" (14). After calculating the "Income Tax" assessment (15), and subtracting this from the net profit before tax, you arrive at your "Net Profit After Tax' (16) figure, and have finished the income statement.

As mentioned previously, an income statement for a manufacturing firm differs slightly from that of a non-manufacturing business; the "Cost of Goods Sold" becomes the "Cost of Goods Manufactured," and this requires a certain amount of detail. In this case (Exhibit 5-2), you must calculate your inventory at the beginning of the accounting period. This includes the "Raw Materials" (3), "Work in Process" (4), and "Finished Inventory" (5). To define these, think of a car manufacturing plant. Raw materials are waiting to be placed on the line, work in process is that being worked on the line, and finished inventory are the cars waiting to go to the show rooms.

To this total (6) must be added the sum of "Purchases" (7), made within the accounting period, the "Direct Labour" (8), that helped to create the product, and the "Factory Overhead" (9) which includes all of the other costs of production. This sum gives subtotal (10); then, by subtracting the "Ending Inventory (12), from (11), the sum of (6) + (10), your "Cost of Goods Manufactured" (2) is calculated. After this, the income statement is identical to that of a non-manufacturing firm.

If accurate records for the business have been kept, the income statement should be fairly easy to tabulate. Greater complexity is faced when a "pro forma income statement" must be calculated. "Pro Forma" literally means, "for the future." When you are estimating the likelihood of profits or losses, you should do pro forma income statements for at least three years. This will give a clear indication of the validity of your operation.

To complete the pro forma income statement requires a certain amount of detective work. First, you will have to estimate your sales. (See section on "Predicting Sales"); then, it is necessary to estimate costs, so that you can calculate your mark-up, and, therefore, the cost of goods sold or manufactured. Next, you will have to calculate all your expenses. The balance of the income statement is just an exercise in filling in the blanks.

This is not an easy process. It is ideal to do three calculations for each time period of your pro forma income statements. These are: 1) pessimistic, 2) realistic, and 3) optimistic assessments of your business potential. By outlining these three possibilities, you will have a far clearer idea about the viability of your enterprise.

An accountant can certainly do these calculations for you, but it is definitely in your best interests to complete the income statement yourself; then, it is often worthwhile to check the calculations with an expert. If you do farm out the work, make certain that you understand completely the derivation of all the numbers; this will ensure that you are making correct business decisions with the resources at your disposal.

Exhibit 5-1

Sample Income Statement
Non-Manufacturing Business

ABC Company
Income Statement: **Year Ending March 15, XXXX**

Gross Sales	$55,000	(1)
Returns and Allowances	1,000	(2)
Net Sales	54,000	(3) = (1) – (2)
Cost of Goods Sold	15,000	(4)
Gross Profit	39,000	(5) = (3) – (4)
Operating Expenses		
Salaries $8,000 (6)		
Rent 15,000 (7)		
Promotion 1,000 (8)		
Transport 500 (9)		
Hydro 300 (10)		
Depreciation 100 (11)		
Miscellaneous 100 (12)		
Total Expenses	25,000	(13) = (6 + 7 + ... +12)
Net Profit Before Tax	14,000	(14) = (5)–(13)
Income Tax	3,000	(15)
Net Profit After Tax	$ 11,000	(16) = (14)–(15)

THE BALANCE SHEET

While the income statement shows how well the business has done over time, the balance sheet demonstrates how the operation is doing at a particular point. This is done by showing the assets, liabilities, and net worth of the business as of a given date.

The balance sheet derives its name from the fact that it must balance; as the total assets always equal the liabilities plus the net worth. The simplest definition of assets is what the business owns. Liabilities are what the business owes. Net worth is the owner's stake in the business.

Exhibit 5-2

Sample Income Statement
Manufacturing Business

Dennison Lifts Ltd.
Income Statement: Year Ending December 31, 2002

Net Sales			$ 150,000	(1)
Cost of Goods Manufactured (2)				
Inventory, December 31, 2001	$ 10,000 (3)			
Inventory	6,000 (4)			
Raw Materials	12,000 (5)			
Finished Inventory			$ 28,000	(6) = (3 + 4 + 5)
Purchases	55,000 (7)			
Direct Labour	12,000 (8)			
Factory Overhead	16,000 (9)			
			83,000	(10) = (7 + 8 + 9)
			111,000	(11) = (10) + (6)
Less: Inventory, December 31, 2002			31,000	(12)
Gross Profit			80,000	(2) = (11) − (12)
			70,000	(13) = (1) −(2)
Operating Expenses				
General and Administrative			9,000	(14)
Selling Expenses			15,000	(15)
			6,000	(16)
Total Expenses			30,000	(17) = (14 +15 +16)
Net Profit Before Tax			40,000	(18) = (13) − (17)
Income Tax			10,000	(19)
Net Profit After Tax			$30,000	(20) = (18) − (19)

To develop your balance sheet — which is not a difficult process — it is imperative that you understand the meanings of other elements on the balance sheet. (See "Exhibit 5-3). "Current assets" are assets that the business expects to turn into cash within one year. They are stated at their present value or cost, whichever is lower; and are listed in order of liquidity: the most liquid items being those that can be turned into cash most quickly. "Cash" is the amount of money that the business has on hand, usually in a bank or trust account. "Accounts Receivable" is the cash that the business expects to receive from customers. On many balance sheets, accounts receivable is followed by "Allowance for Uncollectable Accounts," which is the amount that the owner(s) assume(s) will not be collected from clients. For the novice entrepreneur, it can be difficult to estimate the amount for this account, and the best method of arriving at a figure is often to analyse industry averages and relate them to your business. Once you have been in business for a couple of years, the "Allowance for Uncollectable Accounts" is easier to measure, as you can base the total on past performance. Inventory is the goods on hand for sale and in storage for non-manufacturing firms; for a manufacturer, raw materials, work in process, and other finished products that have not been sold must be included.

Fixed assets are items that will last longer than one year, and items that are to be used in the operation of the business, but are not intended for resale. Fixed assets should be recorded in the books at their original cost, less depreciation, and stated in order of permanence. Examples of fixed assets include: land, buildings, machinery, office equipment, and automobiles. Items are depreciated over time as they lose value due to wear and tear. For example: a car is worth much less after a year on the road than when new.

One area of the balance sheet that is sometimes difficult to grasp is depreciation with regard to a building. A building bought this year for $1,000,000 will be listed next year on the books in many cases for $950,000. This is caused by the five percent depreciation rate allowed by the government. In reality, the building might have increased in value, but because of the accounting principle of conservatism, this lower value will be stated. This can be of particular importance to an individual looking at buying an existing business, as the buyer will have to calculate the present value of the asset, rather than the stated balance sheet value.

The next part of the balance sheet is the liabilities section. "Current Liabilities" are the amount of money that the venture owes, and must pay within one year. These liabilities often include "Accounts Payable," which is money owed to suppliers; "Notes Payable," which is money owed to other lenders; "Accrued Expenses Payable," which is money owed for goods or services; and "Taxes Payable," which is money owed to the government.

"Long-Term Liabilities" are the funds that a business has borrowed and must repay at some point after one year. Common examples of this would be "Notes Payable," which would be the portion of the bank note due after one year; a "First Mortgage Bond," which is a bond that the business might have issued to buy a building.

The last section of the balance sheet is the "Net Worth" portion, also sometimes referred to as "Equity," or in the case of shareholders, "Shareholders' Equity" or "Stockholders' Equity." As stated previously, the net worth is the owner's stake in the business.

For example, say that you purchase a car for $10,000 of which you pay $4,000 in cash and assume a bank loan for $6,000. If you were creating a simple balance sheet for this transaction, it would look like this:

	Assets	**Liabilities**	
Car	$10,000	Bank Loan	$ 6,000
		Equity	
		Equity	4,000
		Total Liabilities	
Total Assets	$10,000	**& Equity**	$10,000

The equity in this case is $4,000, the owner's actual stake in the car. Notice, as with all balance sheets, the assets of $10,000 equal the liabilities plus equity of $10,000.

For a business that has not issued shares, the net worth section of the balance sheet will be fairly simple. The most likely entries would be "Equity," which would be the owner's original stake in the business, and "Retained Earnings," which represents profits earned by the operation and reinvested in the business, rather than paid out to the owners. The retained earnings would be adjusted annually, increasing or decreasing by the profit or loss of the business.

For a business that has shareholders, the net worth section of the balance sheet is slightly more complicated. In this case, "Capital Stock," with "Preferred Shares" and "Common Shares" might also be included. Capital stock is the original investment by the owner(s) plus any additional funding in later years. Preferred shares and/or common shares are the components of this capital stock. Preferred shares deed the owner with preference in receiving dividends ahead of common stock holders, preference in receiving money if the firm is liquidated, and also usually guarantees a fixed dividend. Normally though, preferred shares "carry" no voting rights. Common shares, on the contrary, almost always allow the shareholders to vote, but their dividend is not guaranteed, and they are also the last creditors to receive funds if the firm is liquidated, which usually means that they will receive nothing.

Chart 5-1

Balance Sheet Rules
1. The balance sheet always balances. Assets = Liabilities + Equity.
2. The company name and date at the top.
3. Assets on the left side, liabilities and equity on the right.
4. Current assets are listed first, and then fixed assets. Current liabilities are listed before long-term liabilities.
5. Items are listed in order of liquidity and/or permanence.
6. Items are stated at cost or market value, whichever is lower.

In the same manner as there is a pro forma income statement, there is a pro forma balance sheet, and this will also help you to realize whether or not the firm has the potential for success. The pro forma balance sheet is also derived by making educated estimates. In this case, you will have to gaze into the future, and decide on the numerous transactions in which the firm will engage. This is not a simple process, but by anticipating the assets and liabilities of the firm, along with its equity position, the prospects for your enterprise will be far clearer.

Exhibit 5-3

Sample Balance Sheet

Jimpsol Jumping Jacks Ltd. Balance Sheet April 15, XXXX

ASSETS

Current Assets

Cash		$ 5,000
Accounts Receivable	$22,000	
Less: Allowance for Uncollectable		
Accounts	3,000	19,000
Inventory		8,000
Pre-payments & Deferred Charges		1,000
Total Current Assets		33,000

Fixed Assets

Land		50,000
Building	40,000	
Less: Accumulated Depreciation	10,000	30,000
Office Equipment	8,000	
Less: Accumulated Depreciation	5,000	3,000
Total Fixed Assets		83,000
Total Assets		$116,000

LIABILITIES

Current Liabilities

Accounts Payable	$ 11,000
Notes Payable	8,000
Income Tax Payable	2,500
Total Current Liabilities	21,500

Long-Term Liabilities

Notes Payable	32,000
First Mortgage Bonds	18,500
Total Long-Term Liabilities	50,500
Total Liabilities	72,000

SHAREHOLDERS' EQUITY

Capital Stock	
Preferred Shares	20,000
Common Shares	10,000
Retained Earnings	14,000
Total Shareholders' Equity	44,000
Total Liabilities & Shareholders' Equity	$116,000

CASE 7: JIM'S FIX-IT: PART 1

Jim Jones had a problem. His accountant was asking for an income statement and balance sheet.

"Why don't you do them for me?" Jim queried.

"Be happy to," his chubby little accountant said. "Only it will cost you $250 bucks, thought you might want to save the money."

"I'll try," said Jim, banging down the phone.

The figures he had to work with were these:

He had bought a building in 1999 for $75,000. He still had to pay $40,000, of which $10,000 was due this year.

His bank account contained $12,000. Customers owed him $4,000, but he owed a total of $6,000 to various suppliers. He also owed the government $1,500 in back taxes and the hydro company $400.

Inventory was worth $3,600, office equipment $1,500, although depreciation on the equipment was $1,200.

He leafed through an old accounting book and noticed that he forgot the same one he always did, depreciation on the building. He added on $7,500 to last year's depreciation, a total of $15,000. He also had paid a thousand in goodwill for the company, he remembered.

His sales for the year had been $42,000. His mark-up on cost of goods sold had been 100 percent. Expenses included the building's depreciation, equipment depreciation, salaries of $3,000, hydro of $3,000, a phone bill of $400, and miscellaneous expenses of $900. The tax rate would be 25 percent.

Jim started working all of this out. His balance sheet did not balance, so he called his accountant. "Where'd I go wrong?" "Who is this?" was the response. "It's Jim. Jim Jones."

"Of course," the accountant said after a pause, "I knew that all the time. Let's see. Did you include retained earnings as a balancing number? Remember you have to add this year's profit to the prior retained earnings."

"No. I forgot all about that," Jim said. "Thanks." He checked the prior year's retained earnings, the total of which was $21,750.

After that, Jim finished his balance sheet and income statement. He wants to know if you obtained the same results.

His year-end is January 15, XXXX.

BOOKKEEPING

Some entrepreneurs choose to ignore the bookkeeping aspect of their operation, leaving this for a bookkeeper or accountant. This is unfortunate, as an understanding of the operation's bookkeeping transactions can greatly increase the businessperson's knowledge about the affairs of his enterprise and provide information for future decision-making.

Numerous types of bookkeeping systems can be utilized. The system outlined here is just one of many. Understanding this system will not provide you with enough information to become a bookkeeper, but should create a further understanding of the transactions occurring within your business. While numerous computer programs will make these changes relatively easy to do, it remains important that the methodology behind the numbers is understood.

Debits and Credits

Virtually every business uses a "double-entry" accounting system consisting of debits and credits. "Debit" means the left-hand side of an account; therefore "to debit" means to change the left side. "Credit" means the right-hand side of the account; therefore "to credit" means to change the right side. For every debit transaction, there must be an equal credit transaction. This is the rationale of the double-entry system. Three rules govern this system which are:

1. Increases in assets are debits; decreases are credits.
2. Increases in liabilities are credits; decreases are debits.
3. Increases in equity accounts are credits; decreases are debits.

Credit and debit have nothing to do with value judgments. To credit an account is not necessarily better than to debit an account.

Journals and Ledgers

Most firms keep track of their bookkeeping transactions in the "ledger" on their computer. A ledger is simply a group of accounts. Within this ledger is the "journal," which is the record of all the accounting transactions that must be debited or credited within an accounting period. Within the journal, debits are listed first, with credits indented and following. The act of writing these entries is called "posting."

Let us say that on a regular business day, ABC Ltd. made four transactions. They were as follows:

1) a cash sale for $3,000;
2) a credit sale for $8,000;
3) inventory valued at $10,000 was bought with $4,000 in cash, the rest payable in 30 days;
4) a receivable of $1,000 was collected.

The entries to record each of these transactions would be:

XXXX	Accounts	Debit	Credit
1) July 21	Cash	3,000	
	Sales		3,000
2) July 21	Acc. Rec.	8,000	
	Sales		8,000
3) July 21	Inventory	10,000	
	Acc. Payable		6,000
	Cash		4,000
4) July 21	Cash	1,000	
	Acc. Rec.		1,000

"T" Accounts

After making the initial post, your software program will likely make the other relevant changes for you.

The initial entry in each account is the last total on the balance sheet. For example: Suppose ABC Ltd. had accounts with the following balances: $4,000 in cash; $4,000 in accounts receivable; car for $7,000 and a note payable of $15,000. The opening T accounts for the business would be the following:

Cash		Acc. Rec.		Note Payable	
4000		4000			15000

Car	
7000	

After the four transactions of July 21 were recorded, the T accounts would like this:

Cash		Acc. Rec.		Inventory	
4000		4000		10000	3
3000	1	8000	2	10000	
3	4000	4	1000		
1000	4	11000			
4000					

Sales		Acc. Pay.		Car	
1	3000	3	6000	7000	
2	8000		6000		
	11000				

Note Payable	
	15000
	15000

At the bottom of each account is the total, which represents the difference between the debits and the credits. If these numbers prove to be correct, these totals could then appear on the balance sheet or income statement.

Adjusting Entries

Sometimes entries must be made at the end of the accounting period that are not reflected in the daily transactions of the business. Three examples of this would be: entries for depreciation, for bad debts, and for cost of goods sold. For example: if a car depreciated by $5,000 during an accounting period, the corresponding adjusting entry would be:

Car Depreciation Expense   5000
        Accumulated Depreciation   5000

Car Depr. Exp.		Accum. Depr. Car	
5000	5	5	5000
5000			5000

Another example would be Bad Debt Expense of $2,000. Adjusting entries would be:

Bad Debt Expense   2000
        Allowance for Bad Debts   2000

Bad Debt Exp.		Allow. Bad Debt	
2000	6	6	2000
2000			2000

A third example would be adjusting the inventory for those goods that have been sold.

Cost of Goods Sold   3000
Inventory   3000

C.G.S.		Inventory	
3000	7	7	3000
3000			3000

Closing of Accounts

At the end of each accounting period, the income statement should be "cleared." To do this, each T account is totalled. Next, the adjusting entries are made to the T accounts, and then the resulting figures can be posted to the income statement or balance sheet. The final closing entry to be made requires all revenue and expense accounts to be closed to an account called the "income summary." This will ultimately show the profit or loss for the period. Later, this income summary account is closed to the equity section of the balance sheet, creating the balancing formula. For this example, the final closing entries would be:

Income Summary	5000	
Car Depr. Exp.		5000
Income Summary	2000	
Bad Debt Expense		2000
Income Summary	3000	
C.G.S.		3000
Sales	11000	
Income Summary		11000

Income Summary			Car Depr. Exp.	
5000	8		5000	
2000	9		8	5000
3000	10		0	0
11	11000			
	1000			

Bad Debt Exp.	
2000	
9	2000
0	0

Sales			Cost of Goods Sold	
11000			10	3000
11	11000			3000
0	0			

Net Income would therefore be $1,000 (income summary). A final entry would then be done to the retained earnings.

Net Income   1000
    Retained Earnings   1000

Ret. Earn.			Net Income	
12	1000		1000	12
	1000		1000	

Trial Balance

One partial check to see if the T accounts are correct is to do a trial balance work sheet. This can be done at any point in the business year; it will check if the debits and credits are of equal value. This does not certify that all transactions have been included, or that accounts have been credited and debited correctly. But by doing a trial balance, many errors can be spotted and eliminated.

The trial balance work sheet can vary from the one shown on page 206, particularly for firms with more categories of entries, or that wish to follow certain accounts particularly carefully.

CASE 8: JIM'S FIX-IT: PART TWO

After Jim Jones had completed his income statement and balance sheet, he took them to his chubby accountant's office. Jim noticed how everything in the office was expensive: the Persian rugs, the oak desks, the Picasso paintings on the wall. After sitting and admiring the surroundings for a few minutes, Jim began to estimate what the furnishings would cost. After reaching $387,652.42, the perfectly coiffured secretary interrupted his calculations by saying, "Mr. Jones, Mr. Chubby will see you now."

Jim walked into another spacious room. "Good day, Mr. Jones," Mr. Chubby said.

"Good day, Mr. Chubby," Mr. Jones responded. "Nice office you have here."

Exhibit 5-4

Trial Balance Worksheet

Account	Trial Balance Beginning	Transactions Debit	Transactions Credit	Adjustments Debit	Adjustments Credit	Closing Debit	Closing Credit	Income	Balance
Cash	4000	4000							4000
Acc. Rec.	4000	11000							11000
Note Pay.	15000		15000						15000
Car	7000	7000							7000
Inventory		10000			3000				7000
Sales			11000			11000		11000	
Acc. Pay			6000						6000
Ret. Earn.							1000		
Car Depr. Exp.				5000			5000	5000	
Accum. Depr. Car					5000				5000
Bad Dept Exp.				2000			2000	2000	
Allow. Bad Debt					2000				2000
C.G.S.				3000			3000	3000	
Inc. Sum.						1000		1000	
Net Income							1000	1000	
	15000 = 15000	32000 = 32000		10000 = 10000		12000 = 12000			

"Thank you Mr. Jones," the accountant said with a simpering grin, calculating the vast quantities of money the furnishings had cost. "What can we do for you today?"

Mr. Jones, being a fairly simple man, was not certain who the "we" meant, as only he and Mr. Chubby were in the room. After pondering this, he said politely, "We can check my income statement and balance sheet to see if they are correct."

Mr. Chubby, whose first name was Ernest, examined them for a full two minutes. "Yes, yes, they appear to be quite fine."

"That's wonderful," Mr. Jones said with glee. "I suppose that now that I can do this, I won't need your services any longer."

Mr. Chubby looked concerned. He saw an empty space on the wall and imagined a Tom Forrestall painting there. "Well, really Mr. Jones, do not be so hasty. I think it is time we implemented a bookkeeping system for you."

From the trial balance or T accounts, an income statement and a balance sheet can now be made.

Exhibit 5-5

ABC Ltd.

Income Statement: July 21, XXXX

Net Sales		$11,000
Cost of Goods Sold		3,000
Gross Profit		8,000
Expenses		
Bad Debt Expense	$2,000	
Car Depreciation	5,000	
Total Expenses		7,000
Net Profit Before Tax		$ 1,000

Exhibit 5-6
ABC Ltd. Balance Sheet July 21, XXXX

ASSETS
Current Assets
Cash		$ 4,000
Accounts Receivable	$11,000	
Less: Allowance for Bad Debts	2,000	9,000
Inventory		7,000
Total Current Assets		20,000
Fixed Assets		
Car	7,000	
Less: Accumulated Depreciation	5,000	2,000
Total Fixed Assets		2,000
Total Assets		$22,000

LIABILITIES
Current Liabilities
Accounts Payable	$ 6,000
Total Current Liabilities	6,000
Long-Term Liabilities	
Note Payable	15,000
Total Liabilities	21,000

EQUITY
Retained Earnings	1,000
Total Equity	1,000
Total Liabilities & Equity	$22,000

Keeping accurate books is an important part of operating a business. To learn these skills takes time, but once they are known, the operations of the venture can be more clearly understood. This can aid you in decision-making.

"And how much would that cost?" Mr. Jones asked, the question leaping from his mouth before one could say "diplomacy."
"Hardly anything at all," Mr. Chubby responded. "I suppose that

if you wanted, you could learn to do it on your own. But that would not be easy."

Jim knew that it would be a couple of years more before his firm would be making very much money. "I want to try it," he said, after a moment. "Just to see if I can do it."

"Your choice," said Mr. Chubby. "And remember, you can come crying to me if things don't work out."

Jim decided that he needed an action plan. He determined that he would pick up accounting software on the way home, and keep track of all the transactions for the following week, recognizing that the process was the same for a month or a year.

After returning home, Jim put the ledger under his pillow and quickly fell asleep. He dreamed about journal entries, T accounts, trial balances, adjusting and closing entries, and a final income statement and balance sheet. When he woke up the next morning, he could only think of accounting fun.

The transactions for the week were:

January 22

1) Jim sold $3,000 of goods for cash.

2) He bought a used car for $2,000 cash.

3) He did work on a motor for which he was paid $200 and would receive another $200 the following week.

January 23

4) He paid his employee $400.

5) He paid $1,000 on his bank loan.

January 24

6) He depreciated the rest of his office equipment.

January 25

7) He made another sale for $500 cash.

January 26

8) An old account paid $300.

At the end of the week, Jim sat down at his desk and began working feverishly. He remembered that he would need last year's balance sheet to do some of the work. He referred back to "Jim's Fix-It: Part 1," and then commenced bookkeeping. "Sure glad I closed down last week," Jim told himself, "or who knows how difficult this would be."

What were Jim's results?

Planning Your Cash Flow

The statement that forms the "backbone" of any new business is the cash flow analysis. This is the key projection that aids in the formation of all other statements. Cash flow analysis provides an ongoing picture of when you expect to receive cash, and when that cash must be disbursed to pay the bills. It helps to ascertain when shortages of funds might occur and, therefore, to determine not only how much outside funding you'll need, but when you'll need it. As such, it's an essential tool for developing an effective cash management strategy for your business, whether your venture is new or already operational.

The cash flow statement can also help you in a number of other ways. It will help you to identify your accounts receivable, and thus, motivate you to collect them as soon as possible. Accounts payable are also recorded and appriorized which helps you in paying the bills of suppliers. Lastly, cash flow forces a quantifiable analysis of the development of your organization, which will be a necessity when visiting a bank manager for a loan.

The process of creating a detailed cash flow statement (see "Exhibit 5-5") can be time-consuming, as you must consider all the costs and revenues of the operation as they are incurred. But take heart; once the initial model is created, subsequent efforts will be simplified considerably, since you'll only need to adjust the numbers themselves from time to time, to reflect changing circumstances. In any event, following are the basic steps necessary to create a cash flow statement.

First of all, you must estimate your sales, accounts receivable, and other cash that you will receive for the month, and enter the figures in the appropriate columns under "Cash in". These columns should then be totalled to obtain the "total cash in." Don't forget that particularly during start-ups, there may be a time lag between the time you issue an invoice and the collection time. The lag could be as much as several months, so you may need extra cash reserves to tide you over this period. If you do have such a reserve, or if you intend to take out a loan to cover these initial costs, include this amount in the initial "cash on hand" area at the top of the statement.

If the sale is one hundred dollars and the terms of the sale are 50 percent cash now and 50 percent in two months, then you would place fifty dollars in sales now and the other fifty dollars in accounts receivable two months down the line. You do this because this outlines when you can actually touch the money. This is critical for cash flow analysis: that you are forecasting when you will actually receive and pay the funds.

By adding the "cash on hand" to the "total cash in," the "total cash" figure will be obtained.

Next, you must calculate any cash that you will be disbursing within the month. Typically, this category might include operating costs, such as those for labour (salaries and benefits), material, rent, phone, utilities, stationery and postage, advertising, and loan payments.

If you are using depreciable equipment, it might be wise to make an allowance for these items by dividing the replacement value of the equipment by its anticipated useful lifetime (in months), and including the resulting monthly figure in your expenses. That way, you won't find yourself facing an unexpected replacement bill some time in the future, without having the funds to cover it; you'll have effectively set aside the required funds each month. Of course, the nature of your cash flow may dictate that such funds be set aside, say, quarterly rather than monthly, but the point is that they should be included somewhere in your statement, because these funds for equipment will have to be disbursed eventually.

Similarly, if expansion will necessitate the purchase of additional equipment, then these capital expenditures could be included on your statement. It's possible that you may need to borrow additional funds for this purpose, and lenders will be much more amenable to lending the money if you have predicted this need from the outset.

Also, don't forget to include any funds you may wish to withdraw from the firm, either as your own salary, as dividends, or a repayment for the loans you've made to the business. Once you've developed a clear, month-by-month picture of your expenses, these should be totalled and included in each monthly column, under "total cash out."

From here on, the going is straightforward: take your "total cash out" figure and subtract this amount from your "total cash" to determine the "monthly balance." Add this result to the "cash on hand" for the next month, and continue with the same procedure for succeeding months until you've completed 36 months of cash flow.

After completing these calculations, take your anticipated income and expenses and lump them into three-month periods, using the same columnar format for the subsequent two years, to complete your five-year cash flow statement.

It is also worthwhile to include a "cash flow from operations" figure in your chart. This is derived by subtracting your "total cash out" from "total cash in." This shows if the business is achieving a positive or negative cash flow situation. In almost every case, the more positive this number, the better is the cash flow situation.

If, at some point, you find that the "monthly balance" is a negative number, or is negligibly positive, then you must immediately think of methods to refinance the venture or cut expenses. Otherwise, you might not be able to meet your financial obligations and bankruptcy might ultimately result.

The ideal cash flow plan includes optimistic, realistic, and pessimistic forecasts. By designing three individual plans, utilizing each of these types of predictions, you can prepare contingency actions if operations vary from your most feasible projections. Every four months you should also check to ensure that the cash flow statement is fairly accurate ("Budgeted" versus "Actual"), and update your projections when operations do not follow the forecasted course.

You can improve your cash flow in a number of ways. First, take advantage of discounts offered by suppliers. Usually, these discounts compare favourably with banks' interest rates. If they do, pay your supplier promptly to save cash. But if the supplier offers no discount, wait until the last possible day to make your payment, thereby stretching your accounts payable.

Keep a record of your accounts receivable. Remember, when a customer is tardy paying, give him a call and tell him that his payment is due or, in some cases, overdue. Don't hesitate to apply greater pressure as the period increases.

Another method of improving your cash flow is by establishing a short-term line of credit with a bank. This cash will give you funding to help through difficult times, until your cash flow improves. Refinance your fixed obligations as your banker will allow, and do not borrow a great deal of money all at once to finance major purchases. Spread out these acquisitions, leasing items, if this will improve the cash flow crunch.

If you utilize these techniques, your cash flow position should be greatly enhanced. This will be a major contribution to making your venture a success.

Exhibit 5-7

Cash Flow Worksheet

	Jan.		Feb.		March		April		May		June		July		. . .	
	B*	A**	B	A	B	A	B	A	B	A	B	A	B	A		
Cash on Hand																
Cash In: Sales																
Acc. Rec.																
Other																
Total Cash In																
Total Cash																
Cash Out: Rent																
Labour																
Materials																
Hydro																
Advert.																
Bank Loan																
Other																
Capital Expenditures																
Replacements																
Total Cash Out																
Cash Flow From Operations																
Monthly Balance																

B* — The Budgeted Forecast   A** — The Actual Happening

CASE 9: THE JONSON SAGA: PART 2

Dave and Dolly Jonson were debating the potential for the catering business. "We have almost no money!" Dave insisted for the umpteenth time.

"We've got money," Dolly corrected, "$2,000 that we can use any way we want. Let's use it for this. And we hardly need any money for this business. With our sales in the first few months, the business will carry itself."

"I still don't see where you get those numbers," Dave said. "They just don't make sense to me!"

"Relax," said Dolly, "and I'll show you again. We'll rent Jurgenson's storefront. He said he'll give us a lease for $150 a month for as long as we want."

"But that place is a real dive!"

"I know. I know. But remember that people won't be coming there very often. And he says that if we take it over, he's got a man who will fix it up in February and March for us. He says that it will cost us $1,800 altogether which we can divide between the two months. That means if we start the business in December, we'll just have to work around things a bit. And that won't be difficult."

"I can see how we can work around things easily enough, but it does increase our rent quite a bit."

"But it is still a bargain, and it's the only way he'll rent it to us. Now let me continue. For the first three months, I figure we'll need to buy about $300 of stuff per month. After that, I figure about $900 worth a month. We can mark that up three times and we'll do just fine."

"You mean $300 of goods for each month until the fourth month and then $900 in that month and every month after?"

"That's what I said."

"Just making it clear to myself. And then when are the people going to pay?"

"I've allowed for that. I figure we'll get about 50 percent of the money up front and the rest will come in the following month. Did I mention that we'll sell everything we buy? You know that I am smart that way."

"I'll believe that when I see it. But even if we assume the fifty-fifty rule, and that we will sell everything, it still seems like only a few of our costs."

"Let me finish then. I figure we'll hire one person for about 10 hours a month at $10 an hour. Then we're going to have to do some promotion. I've budgeted $100 for the first month, then $200 for the next two months, and then a hundred a month after that. By then word-of-mouth should boost our sales. Incorporating and all that stuff should cost about $500, and then I guess we'll need utensils. That will cost about $100 to start with. In February, when we get the microwave, I figure we'll need about $400 more of utensils and equipment."

"What about the microwave?"

"Buy it in February for $750."

"It sounds so easy," said Dave, "but I don't really know if it is."

"You're such a worry wart," Dolly scolded playfully. "I'll tell you what. We'll do the numbers together and I'll show you how it works. O.K.?"

"O.K.," agreed Dave.

How does it work?

THE BREAK-EVEN ANALYSIS

One of the best methods to indicate your potential for success in business is to calculate the venture's break-even point. This is the point at which the total costs of the operation equal the total revenues. While you make no profits at this point, you do not suffer any losses either.

The estimation of your break-even point begins by analysing your costs. There are two types of costs to be classified and totalled — fixed and variable. Fixed costs are constant, or the change in these costs is so minimal as to be considered insignificant. Rent is a good example of a fixed cost, as you normally pay a flat fee every month. Your telephone bill might vary slightly from month to month, but generally the difference will be minor, therefore, telephone bills can usually be considered to be fixed costs. A check of your other expenses will lead you to discover other fixed costs.

Variable costs, as the name indicates, vary with revenues. As your sales increase in most businesses, the cost of goods also grows proportionately, therefore, cost of goods sold is an example of a variable cost. Another example is a salesperson on commission; his commission will increase as the sales grow.

The next step in calculating your break-even point is to calculate the "contribution." Contribution is the amount of money remaining after you have subtracted the variable costs from the sales price to offset your fixed costs. You will arrive at the break-even per sales dollar by dividing your fixed costs by your contribution per sales dollar. In a similar vein, to arrive at your break-even point in units, you take the fixed costs and divide them by the contribution per unit.

Two examples will help to illustrate this:

Example 1

Sale Price of Product = $2.00
Variable Costs = $1.25
Fixed Costs = $15,000
What is the break-even in units?

Step 1

Find the contribution.
Selling Price –Variable Costs = Contribution [*]
$2.00 – $1.25 = .75
therefore the contribution = .75

Step 2

Break-Even in Units = Fixed Costs ÷ Contribution Per Unit
= $15,000 ÷ .75
= 20,000 units

This means that in a year, 20,000 units must be sold to break-even. The possibility of reaching this sales level must then be assessed. If the maximum sales potential is 12,000 units a year, then this business is not realistic. But if the 20,000 units does seem realistic, then this calculation should be done again, including the desired salary as a fixed cost. This will indicate the number of units that must be sold to make the desired return. If this number also is realistic, then the potential exists for a thriving enterprise.

---

*See Chart 5-2 for formulas

Example 2

Estimated Sales = $30,000
Variable Costs = $21,000
Fixed Costs = $6,600
What is the break-even in sales volume?

Step 1
First, the contribution per sales dollar must be found. To do this, the variable cost per sales dollar must be calculated.

Variable Cost Per Sales Dollar = $\dfrac{\text{Variable Costs}}{\text{Sales}}$

$$= \dfrac{\$21,000}{\$30,000}$$

$$= 70¢$$

Step 2
Find the contribution per sales dollar.

Contribution
Per Sales $ = $1.00** – Variable Cost Per Sales Dollar
= $1.00– .70¢
= .30¢

Step 3
Break-Even in Sales $ = $\dfrac{\text{Fixed Costs}}{\text{Contribution Per Sales \$}}$

$$= \dfrac{\$6,600}{.30}$$

$$= \$22,000$$

Therefore sales volume of $22,000 is necessary to break-even. Since sales are estimated at $30,000, this enterprise should do quite well.

**$1.00 is always used

Break-Even Graph

Another handy tool that the entrepreneur can utilize to estimate when there will be neither profits nor losses is the break-even graph. For example:

Say that you own a convenience store. Your average mark-up is 100 percent, therefore the variable costs are 50 cents on the dollar. Fixed costs are $10,000 a month. Your average customer spends $3.00. Construct the break-even graph.

Step 1: Construct the axis with "Number of Customers Per Month" on one, and "Monthly Sales Revenues & Costs" on the other.

Step 2: Draw the "Fixed Costs" line, which is parallel to the horizontal axis because it does not vary.

Step 3: Draw the "Total Cost" line, beginning from the $10,000 of fixed expenses, to demonstrate the increase in variable costs.

This line will increase at the rate of $1.50 per customer, as the average customer spends $3.00 and half of this amount is the variable cost.

Step 4: Draw the "Revenue" line, beginning at $0, showing the sales increase of $3.00 per customer. The point at which the "Total Cost" and "Revenues" lines cross is the break-even point. At this point the total costs and total revenues are equal.

By careful analysis of this graph, you can see what the profit or loss will be at different sales levels. This is an excellent aid as you plan your business and estimate your potential sales volume.

Of course, the object of beginning your business is not to break even, but to achieve a profit. But knowledge of the sales and unit volume necessary to achieve the break-even point can help tremendously in your assessment of the viability of your potential venture.

Graph 5-1
Break-Even Graph

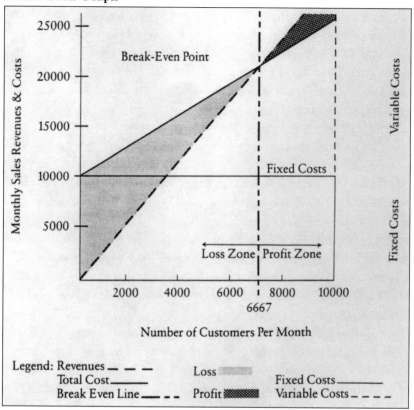

Chart 5-2

Break-Even Formulas

1. Contribution Per Unit = Selling Price - Variable Cost Per Unit
2. Break-Even in Units = $\dfrac{\text{Fixed Costs}}{\text{Contribution Per Unit}}$
3. Contribution Per Sales $ = $1.00 - Variable Cost Per Sales $
4. Break-Even in Sales $ = $\dfrac{\text{Fixed Costs}}{\text{Contribution Per Sales \$}}$
5. Variable Cost Per Sales $ = $\dfrac{\text{Variable Costs}}{\text{Sales}}$
6. Contribution = Sales - Variable Costs
   Break Even: Total Costs = Total Revenues

CASE 10: A CASE ON WOOD AND STUFF

Clarence, after combing his hair once more, checking his face carefully in the mirror, and adjusting his jacket, told Bill, "So, we just buy the firewood for forty-five bucks a cord, break it into ten packages and presto! sell them for ten buckarooskies each. No problem at all! The delivery truck will cost us about ten cents a kilometre and we'll have to drive about three hundred kilometres a month. Plus, we'll hire three guys for a couple hundred a month each to do a bit of pulling and delivering and all that stuff. Three hundred dollars of advertising a month and that should do it for us."

"We'll need some bags to put the wood in," Bill said. "Those will run about fifty cents for each bag we deliver. And new saw blades will cost us about twenty bucks a month. It won't be as cheap as you think."

"C'mon Billy Boy. We'll be running the dough before you can say 'timber'." "What I want to know, Clarence, is how many cords we'll have to sell a month to break-even. And then I want to know how much we'll have to sell to make a thousand bucks a month each, in both dollars and cords."

"A thousand bucks a month! A thousand bucks a month! Gee, Billy Boy, that's not even scraping the surface. We'll be bloody millionaires soon."

"You always think too big, Clarence. That's why you've gone bankrupt four times. No, you just answer me those questions and then I'll decide if I want to get involved."

RATIO ANALYSIS

One area of business analysis that is often ignored or avoided by small business people is ratio analysis. Ratio analysis can provide a wealth of information for the entrepreneur, information that can establish the groundwork for the majority of future business decisions.

Ratio analysis indicates where the business has been, where the business is now, and can illustrate where the business is heading. By taking the time to examine the balance sheets and income statements of the operation, and by working through the following equations, the entrepreneur can discover or verify weaknesses within his operation and take the necessary steps to correct these deficiencies. Conversely, strengths will be found, solidified, and acted upon in the future operations of the enterprise.

A ratio analysis should be done at least once a year. This procedure will help to ensure that the business is being properly monitored and that the activities of the business are compatible with its financial position.

A) Liquidity Ratios

The liquidity ratios demonstrate how easily the firm can turn its debts into cash and, therefore, pay accounts as they become due. This is critical, for a business that cannot pay its debts will soon find itself in bankruptcy.

1) Working Capital

Working capital demonstrates the amount of money the business has on hand to pay its debts by calculating the difference between the current assets and current liabilities. Because it is the current portion of the balance sheet that is being evaluated, this ratio indicates the working capital requirements for the upcoming year.

Working Capital = Current Assets – Current Liabilities

---

2) Current Ratio

The current ratio, like the working capital ratio, compares the firm's assets with its current liabilities, but instead of putting them in dollar figures, it utilizes a true ratio format. Though standards vary from industry to industry, a healthy current ratio is generally considered to be 2:1. This means that the business should be able to cover what it owes in the upcoming twelve months, twice.

Current Ratio = Current Assets: Current Liabilities

When analysing ratios, it is worthwhile to examine the trend to see if it is positive or negative. For example:

ABC Company	2002	2003	2004
Current Assets	$80000	90000	100000
Current Liabilities	40000	70000	100000
Current Ratio	2:1	1.29:1	1:1

These figures show a negative trend as the 2:1 in 2002 is a healthy ratio, and this decreases to 1:1 in 2004. The analysis should then lead one to examine the current portion of the assets and liabilities on the balance sheet, and to determine which factors are causing the difficulties; then corrective action can be taken. This type of analysis is critical for all of the ratios. For an individual who does not have a number of years to work with, this type of comparison is impossible, and the analysis would then have to be made in accordance with industry standard, which can be found in reference books at the library.

3) Acid Test Ratio

This ratio is exactly the same calculation as for the current ratio except that you do not include the inventory. There are two major reasons for determining this ratio. The first is that inventory is often difficult to liquidate quickly. Secondly, if it is liquidated quickly, there is a tremendous likelihood that the seller will only receive a percentage of his payment price. In some respects, therefore, this is a truer measure of the liquidity of a business than the current ratio.

Acid Test = (Current Assets – Inventory): Current Liabilities

4) Debt to Equity Ratio

This ratio illustrates the amount "invested" in the business by creditors, as compared to the investment by the owner. The higher this ratio is, the larger the creditors' claim on the business. The major danger here occurs if the creditors' portion becomes so high the business cannot pay the debt, or creditors demand their money.

Philosophically, there is a major business debate involved here — that of conservatism versus risk and leverage. The higher the debt to equity ratio, the greater the business' leverage. This leverage is the result of the fact that the operation is utilizing other people's money to make a profit, rather than the equity of the owners. Greater leverage means the potential for a higher return on investment. (See "Return on Investment" ratio). It also often means a greater chance for bankruptcy.

There is not an ultimate answer as to whether one should be a conservative operator or engage in high leverage practices. Many extremely successful corporations are completely averse to debt and finance everything internally. Alternatively, numerous major corporations have high debt to equity ratios and remain successful. One consideration here is your banker. In times of difficulty, or perhaps recession or depression, will the banker be ready to "pull the plug" on businesses that owe a lot of money? In the past recession, many enterprises went bankrupt for this very reason: a high debt to equity ratio and a nervous banker.

$$\text{Debt to Equity} = \frac{\text{Long-Term Debt}}{\text{Equity}}$$

5) Age of Accounts Receivable

The age of accounts receivable ratio demonstrates how many days on average it takes for the business to collect on a sale. This is a critical ratio, as one of the reason businesses fail is that clients take an unreasonable amount of time to pay, or do not pay at all. Entrepreneurs must make certain that they obtain their receivables as quickly as possible.

$$\text{Age of Accounts Receivable} = \frac{\text{Accounts Rec.}}{(\text{Sales} \div 365^{*})}$$

6) Age of Accounts Payable

This ratio demonstrates how long, on average, it takes you to pay for the things you buy. There is an interesting balance here. On the one hand, it is worthwhile to "stretch accounts payable." This means that by paying more slowly, you maintain cash for a longer period of time and, therefore, can use the funds in the business or to earn interest at the bank. Conversely, if you stretch accounts payable too much, suppliers might become disenchanted with you, and treat you shabbily — or worse — cut off your credit and supplies.

$$\text{Age of Accounts Payable} = \text{Acc. Pay.} \div (\text{Purchases} \div 365)$$

*365 is used as it is the number of days in a year. Some businesses choose to use 360 or another number.

7) Age of Inventory

The age of inventory indicates how many days it takes to turn over the goods for sale. Ideally, inventory turnover should be as often as possible while avoiding stock-outs that might discourage the return of customers, and minimizing the cost of supplies.

$$\text{Age of Inventory} = \text{Inventory} \div (\text{C.G.S.} \div 365)$$

B) Profitability Ratios

As the name suggests, profitability ratios indicate the profitability of the enterprise. Remember, it is important to compare the current result to prior years to see if the trend is positive or negative. This will help in the production of an action plan to improve the situation.

1) Gross Profit to Sales

The gross profit to sales ratio demonstrates the difference between the cost of goods sold and their selling price. If the percentage is increasing, this indicates that the selling price has increased, or that one or more elements in the cost of goods calculation has decreased. This change could be the result of a company buying more astutely, of high labour productivity, or perhaps of a lower plant overhead. If a negative situation is noted, corrective action should be undertaken.

$$\text{Gross Profit to Sales} = \frac{\text{Gross Profit}}{\text{Sales}}$$

2) Net Profit to Sales

This ratio demonstrates the percentage of each dollar of sales that becomes profit. It should be analyzed in conjunction with the gross profit to sales ratio. For example, if the gross profit to sales is increasing and net profit to sales is decreasing, this indicates that the firm might be losing control of their expenses. In this instance, expenses should be carefully analysed to see which ones are increasing and whether this increase is justifiable.

> Net Profit to Sales = $\dfrac{\text{Net Profit}}{\text{Sales}}$

3) Return on Investment (R.O.I.)

The return on investment illustrates the percentage payback that the owners are receiving on their equity in the business. This equity is equivalent to the owner's original investment, plus the retained earnings that the venture has generated since its inception.

For many investors, the return on investment ratio is the one that will be analysed first to see if funds are being used wisely. For example, if you are operating a business and the R.O.I. is three percent, and an option is to place your money in the bank at a guaranteed rate of nine percent, the latter would likely be the more attractive investment. By choosing the bank option, you would save working time, receive a higher return on your funds, and eliminate the risk of financial loss through business failure.

Generally, if another company in the industry has a higher R.O.I. over a prolonged period of time, then they are probably doing a more efficient job of operating their business. This state of affairs should lead the management of the laggard to analyse operations and improve their current business practices.

> R.O.I. = Net Profit $\div$ $\dfrac{(\text{Total Equity} + \text{Total Equity})}{2^{*}}$
> Year 1 $\quad\quad$ Year 2

C) *Growth Ratios*

Growth ratios indicate how quickly the business is developing. Many people assume that because an enterprise is growing quickly, it is successful. This is not necessarily the case. Often the growth of a firm is brisk, but its other ratios are such that bankruptcy looms near, therefore, do not rely strictly on growth as an indicator of success.

1) Sales Growth

This shows, quite simply, how quickly sales are growing. The ratio is derived by taking the sales increase this year and dividing it by last year's sales.

*2 — for two years

$$\text{Sales Growth} = \frac{(\text{Sales This Year} - \text{Sales Last Year})}{\text{Sales Last Year}}$$

2) Profit Growth

This illustrates how quickly profit is growing. It should be analyzed with sales in mind. If sales have doubled in the past year, and profit has increased by only twenty percent, problems are indicated.

$$\text{Profit} = \frac{(\text{Net Profit This Year} - \text{Net Profit Last Year})}{\text{Growth Profit Last Year}}$$

3) Asset Growth

This shows how quickly the business is acquiring assets. Usually an increase is a positive trend, unless the owners are investing money foolishly, or the accounts receivable is not being controlled.

$$\text{Asset Growth} = \frac{(\text{Assets This Year} - \text{Assets Last Year})}{\text{Last Year's Assets}}$$

4) Debt Growth

Debt can be assumed by a firm for two primary reasons. The first is for growth, and unless the expansion is too rapid, this can be a wise decision. The second reason for acquiring new debt is mismanagement. Analysis of the debt growth ratio can help to distinguish whether the debt is worthwhile or dangerous. This ratio should be considered with the debt/equity ratio.

$$\text{Debt} = \frac{(\text{Total Debt This Year} - \text{Total Debt Last Year})}{\text{Growth Last Year's Debt}}$$

Ratio analysis is a wonderful tool to utilize when examining and planning your business. When this technique is first encountered, it often seems difficult and, therefore, many people choose to avoid this area. But after just a few hours of work, the mysteries of ratio analysis should begin to disappear, and you should be able to apply the methodology of this chapter.

CASE 11: JILL'S CRAFTS

Your cousin, Jill Friendly, approaches you asking for advice on operating her business. She wants to know specifically, "How can I make more profit?" but she also adds, "And I want to know just how you think things have been progressing so far." You tell her that you will get back to her next week, finish your cheesecake and coffee, and head home.

Comparative Income Statements Year Ending June 30	2000	2001	2002
Net Sales	$8000	12000	19000
Cost of Goods Sold	2000	2800	4000
Gross Profit	6000	9200	15000
Operating Expenses:			
Wages	—	2000	4000
Rent	—	300	1500
Hydro	—	200	300
Transport	50	50	100
Promotion	100	200	300
Total Operating Expenses	150	2750	6200
Net Profit	$5850	6450	8800

Jill's Crafts Comparative Balance Sheet November 30	2000	2001	2002
ASSETS			
Current Assets Cash	$2000	4000	1000
Accounts Receivable	1000	3000	1100
Inventory	2000	5000	9000
Total Current Assets	5000	12000	21000
Fixed Assets			
Machinery	1000	800	600
Total Fixed Assets	1000	800	600
Total Assets	6000	12800	21600

LIABILITIES

Current Liabilities

Accounts Payable	1000	3000	8000
Wages	—	500	1000
Income Tax	—	1000	1000
Total Current Liabilities	1000	4500	10000
Long-Term Liabilities			
Note Payable	—	3300	6600
Total Long-Term Liabilities	—	3300	6600
Total Liabilities	1000	7800	16600
Equity	5000	5000	5000
Total Liabilities & Equity	$6000	12800	21600

PART VI

Now you have arrived at the point where you can prepare a business plan. The business plan is a written outline of the overall objectives and activities of the business enterprise. It will force you to focus on every aspect of your venture, pinpointing potential weaknesses and calculating all of the organization's resources to fulfil both short- and long-term needs. Novice entrepreneurs tend to be overly optimistic about their prospects, but the business plan quantifies projected operating results, often dispelling unwarranted optimism with hard realism. In addition, of course, a business plan is essential when a businessperson wishes to attract investors or obtain a loan from a bank.

Cash flow planning, break-even analysis, pro forma income statements, and balance sheets must all be completed in the process of drawing up the plan. Many novice entrepreneurs find numerical calculations difficult; they therefore attempt to ignore the quantitative area. Unfortunately, to plan adequately and maintain a business, numerical calculations are absolutely essential, and the more financial basics you can understand, the better your chances for success. Avoiding these numerical calculations almost inevitably leads to a business failure. (I know that you've read this before, but for those of you who skipped the numerical section, this is your second and final warning!)

Customers, pricing policy, and competition must also be considered in the business plan: Who will buy the product? Where else can they get it? How much are they willing to pay?

Will you be able to compete? No business start-up is feasible until these questions are answered. In order to do so, you'll have to get down to production details as well: How many employees and how much will they be paid? What about benefits or the potential for union organization? The size of the office, branch plants, and other necessary facilities will also need to be established in the process of determining costs.

Finally, a well-developed business plan will give you a blueprint for ensuring your original projections are being met and, if not, to make the necessary organizational corrections. Often novice entrepreneurs go to all the trouble of drafting a plan, then choose to disregard it claiming, "I haven't got the time to check performance against it," or,

"Things never work out according to plan anyway." These individuals often end up as a statistic — one of the approximately 80 percent of new businesses that close within five years.

Drafting the Plan

There are many ways to structure a business plan, but the actual content is similar, regardless of the manner in which it is organized. Typically, a plan will consist of an introductory page, followed by an executive summary, and table of contents. After this comes the "meat" of the plan: background, management, operations, research and development, marketing, and finance.

Introductory Page

The introductory page includes the name, address, and phone number of the business, and a contact person with a number where she can be reached. It should have a paragraph describing the nature of the business and the intended market area. If business loans or investors are being sought, this should also be mentioned at the outset of the plan.

Executive Summary

The summary highlights the key components of the business plan, including the nature of the business, the desired market, and the key success variables for the business. Projected financial results should also be mentioned here. This would include the estimated sales level, the predicted profit or loss figure, and any business loans that you are seeking. The summary should be fairly short — no more than three pages in length.

Table of Contents

The purpose of the table of contents is simply to make referring to the plan as easy as possible for the reader. In certain cases, this will only be of concern to the owners and any advisors who review the plan; but if a loan is necessary, this will simplify the plan for a banker or other investor. The actual contents of the plan may vary somewhat, depending on the exact nature of the business, but the key areas of any plan are as follows:

Background

Business plans are prepared by two types of people: those who are proposing to enter a business, and those who have been operating for a number of years. While the former group is likely planning the operational blueprint for the first time, the latter group might simply wish to reanalyse the business, or perhaps need a business plan to seek funding from a bank, venture capitalist, or other investor. In either of these cases, the background section should start with a history of the business. If it is a new venture, your own credentials, particularly as they relate to management, should be outlined. And regardless of whether the business is new or established, the reasons for entering the business should be discussed.

Next, check your personal goals. If you don't already own a business, do you really want to be your own boss, and will you sacrifice current income for potential rewards later? What do you want to be doing in five years?

Next, analyse your corporate goals. What size of company do you want? Are you interested in expansion and diversification? How much money can the operation make?

Next, see if the personal and corporate goals mesh. One of the major concerns here is financial requirements. Let's say that you are currently earning $40,000 a year and wish to maintain that standard of living. If the business will not permit a salary for two years, as losses persist or profits are reinvested in the company, and if you do not have a nest egg to fall back on, your personal and corporate goals are not compatible.

Or perhaps you wish to have a large corporation, but really do not have the personal desire to discipline yourself to work hard and deal with employees. Once again, personal and corporate goals do not match, and the business does not appear feasible.

Assuming your personal and corporate goals are compatible, you should now answer the question: "What business am I entering?" This forces you to examine every aspect of the business from the ground up. It also sets the stage for the main element of the business plan — strategy. For a strategy, you should examine the five fundamentals of the operation: management, operations, research and development, marketing, and finance.

Management

The ability of management to operate the business, and reach the desired goals and objectives of the firm should be highlighted in this section. What key personnel are required, and where are they to be found? If, for example, you're opening a furniture factory, you'll probably need a plant manager skilled at running such an operation, a salesperson with the contacts necessary to sell the product, a financial manager, and various support personnel. A resume should be provided for each key person, outlining their education, relevant experience, and the reasons that person would be willing to join the organization. You'll need to give some thought as to how much salary the personnel will want.

Also, the timing and need for future management should be highlighted, as you plan up to five years ahead. This will help to fulfil the time frame of the business plan, as it assesses both short- and long-term needs.

Bankers, venture capitalists, and other sources of capital, also usually wish to see a statement explaining why members of the management group left their former employment. In addition to this, contingency plans should be outlined, in case a management person chooses to leave the organization.

If the business will be of sufficient size, an organizational diagram should be included, outlining the responsibilities of the various management personnel; and the chain of command throughout the enterprise.

Operations

This section should outline all aspects of the day-to-day activities of the enterprise. Often it is best, when preparing this section, to think of every operational facet of the business that you could be involved in on any given day.

Areas to be discussed include the following: staff (other than key management personnel); facilities; equipment requirements and production procedures; suppliers; inventory and distribution; as well as any special considerations that might apply.

How many employees will be required, and how much will they be paid? What about benefits? Profit sharing? Is there a possibility of union involvement? Will training be required, and if so, how will it be provided and how long will it take? As with management, consider additional staff requirements resulting from business growth.

What equipment will be required? How much will it cost? Where can it be obtained? Is the purchase of used equipment a feasible alternative? Perhaps leasing should be considered? How long will the equipment last before it needs to be replaced, and what about expanded requirements?

How large a facility is required? If the venture is in the service sector, you may be able to operate from your basement or an extra bedroom, but if you're going into production, you may need substantial floor space for production, as well as storage and office space. The production process should be explained, with production capabilities and targets analysed. Procedures should be outlined as completely as possible, and a floor plan will probably be required to illustrate work and material flows, and to enhance production efficiencies.

Where should the facility be located? This may not be so critical if you're producing a product that is easily shipped (although it's usually prudent to locate as close to the centre of the market as possible). But if you're opening a store, then location may be of paramount consideration. Will you buy, rent, or build, and how much will it cost in that specific location?

How much inventory will be needed? Will the inventory levels vary from season to season as your turnover rate changes? What methods are going to be set in place to control the inventory flow? Who will your suppliers be? Are you checking for various appropriate suppliers so that you will not have to rely on an individual company? Is there a potential for volume discounts by utilizing fewer suppliers?

What sort of insurance would be most logical for your organization? How will your organization cope with risk? Where should the coverage be obtained from?

What will you do if operations don't work according to your plans? What sort of contingency plans have you outlined? Which critical external factors could cause your business hard ship? Would strikes, recession, weather, a competitor's reaction, or other factors, necessitate a change in your operational plan? By thinking in terms of, "What if ... ?" you will have helped create a plan that will reduce your overall risk.

Research and Development

The majority of novice entrepreneurs do not have to include this section in their business plan, but for those dealing with an invention or innovation, this area is critical for success. The plan must explain why production is merited, discussing every phase from the creation of the prototype, to the purchase of the final product by the consumer. Patent protection must be analysed and costs closely scrutinized. The competitive nature of the marketplace, although also discussed in marketing, must be included here, as it is of major strategic importance for a new product or service.

Marketing

This is a critical but often poorly considered element in the success of many new ventures. The marketing section should begin with an "industry scan," giving an overview of the marketplace. Who are the potential purchasers of your goods or services? Why will they buy your product? Is the market in a growth, mature, or declining stage? What is the current and future size of this market? Who are your major competitors and how are they likely to react to your business? What advantages does your product or service have over competitors? Or perhaps, yours is a new product for an as-yet-untapped market? If this is the case, what market research have you done to guarantee consumer acceptance? Describe any recent or likely major changes in the market, including the impact of new technology if applicable. Mention any major customers that you have contacted, along with their responses to your offerings. Your basic marketing philosophy should also be described.

Next, you should divide your marketing section into the "Four P's" of the marketing mix: Place, Price, Promotion, and Product, and discuss each of these areas in detail.

Remember, marketing is essentially a four-dimensional puzzle with distinct interrelationships between the quality and uniqueness of the product, its price, the target purchasers and the channels by which the product can be provided to them, and the means by which it's brought to their attention. A change in one element will affect all the others.

Finance

The "numbers" end of things may be dry, distasteful, and time-consuming, but there's no avoiding it. You simply must analyse the monetary aspects of the business in tremendous detail to ensure it will fly. Virtually nobody invests in belief alone — particularly not bankers and other institutional lenders; the first thing they'll insist on seeing are your financial statements. These statements should include cash flow projections, break-even analyses, balance sheets, and income statements.

The cash flow statement should be done on a month-by-month basis for two years, and quarterly thereafter. Typically, lenders want to see projections for the next five years, although you may be able to get away with three years. But remember, the further that you can realistically plan for the future, the clearer focus you will have on your business.

The break-even analysis will help you to assess if you can realistically generate enough sales to keep the business running. Often, once this is done, the realization occurs that the venture is not viable and, therefore, the operation must be changed; or perhaps, self-employment is not the answer. While doing this analysis, it is important to divide your costs into their fixed and variable components. This will give you a more lucid indication of potential alternatives if plans must be changed.

Pro forma balance sheets and income statements should also be done for a minimum of three years, and if possible, for five years. If the business has been operating, financial lenders will also wish to see your past statements for as far back as five years.

The financial section of the plan should also highlight any current loans that you or your business have outstanding. If currently applying for a new loan, the amount, terms, and time requirements of the loan should be described, along with an appropriate payback plan. Also a description of the exact purpose of the loan, be it for working capital purposes, to buy a particular piece of equipment, or perhaps to finance a building, should be outlined.

The accounting policies that your business will utilize, depreciation treatment, recognition of obsolete inventory, bad debts, research and development expenses, along with any expected or potential government assistance should also be cited.

When preparing a business plan, you must utilize three scenarios to realize a true picture of your enterprise: optimistic, pessimistic, and realistic. This is especially critical of the financial section. If your income projection under the most optimistic situation is $15,000 per annum and you want to realize $30,000 per annum from the business venture to make it worthwhile, look for another business. But if under the most pessimistic scenario, profit is about $5,000 and that would be adequate for your needs and desires, then you have a potentially viable operation. Above all, though, don't kid yourself with unwarranted optimism.

Do not hesitate to illustrate the negative factors associated with your business when formulating the plan. By mentioning and analysing these factors, you will be better prepared to combat difficulties. A banker or investor should recognize that by facing potential problems, you will have thought through your business carefully and minimize the difficulties as they occur. This is a superior technique to presenting a rosy plan, devoid of any dilemma; such a proposal will likely engender cynicism on the part of any astute banker or investor.

After you have finished the business outline, show it to friends and associates. Listen to their ideas and recommendations, and then change the plan if you decide that it's incomplete or some of the assumptions are unrealistic.

Once the finishing touches are applied and operations have commenced, refer back to the plan to ensure that you are actually following the blueprint you worked so hard to complete. If operations are not working out as you projected, see if you can utilize any new information to achieve better results. By continually updating the business plan to include current market conditions, and by adjusting your goals and objectives as necessary, you should remain in tune with the marketplace, which can only benefit your sales and ultimately your profit potential.

Chart 6-1

Business Plan Chart
1) Introduction Page
2) Executive Summary
3) Table of Contents
4) Background
5) Management

6) Operations
7) Research and Development
8) Marketing
9) Finance

THE BUSINESS PLAN CHECK LIST   YES   NO

1. Introductory Page:
   A) Did you state your business name, with an accompanying address and telephone number? Did you mention a contact person with a telephone number?

   B) Did you briefly describe the nature of the business with an accompanying brief description of the market area?

   C) Did you state any loans or investments sought?

2. Executive Summary
   A) Did you describe in greater detail the nature of the business and the intended market area?

   B) Have you defined your key success variables?

   C) Have you stated your expected sales and profit totals?

   D) Did you describe any loans or investments sought and their purpose?

3. Table of Contents
   Have you created a reference table for the business plan clearly so that readers can easily find the section(s) that they are interested in?

4. Background

A) Have you adequately discussed the history of the business?

B) Did you state why you have chosen to enter the business and briefly mention your credentials?

C) Have you defined both your personal goals and the business goals? Have you checked to see that these goals are compatible?

5. Management

A) Have you discussed management's ability to reach the desired goals?

B) Did you discuss your key personnel requirements, providing a resume for each of these people that includes their education, relevant business experience, personal interests, why they left their previous employment, and why they wish to join your organization? Did you state the expected salary of these individuals?

C) Did you discuss your future needs for management and contingency plans in case existing management leaves your organization?

D) Have you created an organizational diagram outlining responsibilities and the chain of command?

6. Operations

A) Have you completely considered your staffing requirements, an appropriate pay and benefit package, and any necessary training for employees?

B) Have you considered your long-term staffing requirements?

C) Have you considered the possibility of a unionized staff?

D) Have you decided on your equipment needs and the accompanying costs? Have you carefully considered the expected length of service of the equipment?

E) Did you examine your facility needs, the production process, and the location that is best to satisfy these areas? Have you considered your inventory requirements, storage facilities, seasonal variations in demand, and an inventory control system?

F) Have you contacted suppliers and decided on which ones will be best?

G) Have you carefully considered your insurance needs and policies?

H) Have you prepared contingency plans if some of your assumptions remain unfulfilled or difficulties appear?

7. Research and Development
A) Have you clearly examined the need for production and the production process?

B) Has the competitive nature of the marketplace and your position within that marketplace been carefully analysed? Are patents necessary for your product?

8. Marketing

A) Have you done an industry scan, describing the clientele, the market trends, and your competitors?

B) Have you mentioned customers that you have signed to contracts and other sales that appear promising?

C) Did you adequately consider the place component of the marketing mix, discussing your target market and your intended methods of distribution?

D) Have you carefully considered an ideal pricing scheme for your product or service that takes into account competition, market demand, your costs, and the elasticity of pricing?

E) Have you carefully considered the products' quality and packaging?

F) Has your promotional budget been outlined and appropriate media selected?

G) Have you considered ways to obtain free publicity?

H) Have you explained the reason for choosing your business name?

9. Finance

A) Have you completed cash flow projections on a monthly basis for two years and quarterly thereafter utilizing optimistic, pessimistic and realistic scenarios?

B) Have you calculated your break-even point?

C) Are pro forma balance sheets and income statements completed for five years? Do you have past statements to show lenders or investors?

D) Have you outlined any loans outstanding, their amount and terms? Have you outlined the needs for a new loan or investment with appropriate payback scheme? Have you described what the money will actually be used for?

E) Have you documented your accounting policies, your recognition of obsolete inventory, bad debts, research and development expenses, and potential government funding?

F) Have you carefully discussed problems that you are fairly certain the business will face and discussed potential solutions?

CONCLUSION

Starting and operating a successful small business is extremely difficult, which is why approximately half of new businesses do not survive the first two years. The purpose of this book has been to teach methods of evaluating the viability of a prospective enterprise, so that if operations are commenced, the venture will prosper.

Especially in the initial stages of the enterprise, the hours are long, the hardships are constant. But if the idea is sound, the product or service good, and your resolve to succeed great, the rewards of both a monetary and non-monetary nature will make the effort worthwhile.

For those of you considering starting your own business, I hope that this guide has moved you a step closer to realizing that dream.

APPENDIX I
CASE SOLUTIONS

CASE ONE: THE DECISION

Problem
Should Jon start his own outdoor store?

Sub-Problem
Is there a market for the business?

Analysis
There are a number of key factors in this case. These include:

1. Jon has experience in retail, acquired through 12 years of working for a major department store in various capacities. He has worked in the outdoor goods section, the field in which he is considering opening his business.
2. Jon appears to be a diligent, hard-working individual. This is a necessity to operate a small business successfully.
3. Jon appears to get along well with people. He is liked by his staff, and appears to be respected in the community, as both landlords would be happy to have him as a tenant.
4. Jon's financial situation is uncertain; if he leaves his job, odds are that the family will not have an income until Bette returns to work, as most businesses lose money in their first year or two of operation.
5. Jon has not done any market research. Because of his experience in the selling field, and his "intuitive" sense of what would sell, additional research might not be necessary.
6. Jon enjoys his work, but is becoming restless. A promotion to the head office in Vancouver seems to be a possibility, but though this job would present new challenges, Jon was not excited about the prospect of moving.

7. Jon has the support of his family. This is very important for business success.

Alternatives

A) Jon can stay where he is, continuing to work as the store manager. The possibility of growing dissatisfaction with the position exists.

B) Jon can stay in his position and hope for a promotion. But then he would have to move to Vancouver, a possibility that does not appeal to him.

C) Jon can start the business now. This would severely curtail the current earning power of the family, perhaps placing them in a precarious financial position.

D) Jon can bide his time and wait for Bette to return to work, then reconsider opening his store or re-evaluate the promotion if it is offered. This would guarantee a continuous flow of money to support the family.

Recommendations

Jon is the perfect example of an individual who has the potential to be extremely successful in business. He has the necessary job experience, knows the community needs, and appears to get along well with people. However, to open a business now might lead to financial hardship, especially with three young children, a mortgage, and no immediate source of income.

As Jon continues to enjoy his work, I suggest that he remain with the department store until Bette is ready to return to the work force, and then he should reconsider starting the business, or accept the promotion if it is offered. This would appear to be in about 15 months time, one year after their next child is born. By waiting, a continuous flow of income to the family would be ensured. In this way, Jon would be able to serve both his family and personal needs, for both the shorter and longer term.

In addition to the above, Jon might consider doing some market research to evaluate more completely if the store is feasible, although with his experience, the research might actually prove redundant.

CASE TWO: HOT DOGS!!!

Problem
Has Steve planned the business well?

Sub-Problems
1. Steve's character.
2. The sources for financing.
3. The seasonal aspects of the business.
4. The forming of a corporation.

Analysis
1. Steve was late for work six times in a month. This makes it questionable whether he would have the discipline to go to work every day, when there was no boss to push him.
2. Steve received financing from friends. This was probably his only viable option, as professional agencies would have demanded that Steve invest some funds in the business himself. This would have been impossible because he was broke.
3. Steve was starting the business in the fall, as ski season was approaching. This means that in the near future — given Montreal's winters — that Steve will be out of a job. Steve has ignored the seasonal nature of his business.
4. Steve formed a corporation for tax advantages and to limit his liability. Though these are often valid reasons to incorporate, these reasons do not apply to his business, as it will not be making sufficient money.

Alternatives
1. Steve can attempt to work through the Montreal winter. This is unrealistic given both the climate and Steve's personality.
2. Steve could fold the enterprise. This would not make his partners happy.
3. Steve can try to sell the enterprise, although it is unlikely that there are many people dumb enough to buy a business such as this at this time of year.
4. Steve can work until the weather changes, fold the enterprise for the winter, and then recommence operations in the

spring. This option would satisfy both shorter and longer term opportunities.

Recommendations

Steve Berger is an ideal candidate for a business failure for the following reasons:

A) He has ignored his business's seasonal cycle and started the venture at virtually the worst time of the year;

B) He appears to lack the discipline to operate a business;

C) He has wasted his business's limited financial resources by incorporating when this was foolish.

Steve has probably obtained financing from his only viable option: friends. Bankers, government, venture capitalists, etc. would never finance Steve. The most unfortunate aspect of this situation is that Steve s friends will probably lose their money and, because of this, it is possible that Steve will lose his friends. This is the real danger of using this source of financing.

Steve's best chance for success would have been to start the business in the spring. Since he did not do this, his best option at present is alternative number four. But considering Steve's entrepreneurial skills, he will probably not choose this option, and the venture will fail.

CASE THREE: HERBERT'S DECISION

Problem

What should Herbert do?

Sub-Problems

1. Will Herbert like the big city?
2. Can Herbert get along in the big city with his temperament?

Analysis
Choice I: The Empty Store

A) The store seems to be well located for both business and residential clientele.

B) The cost is $250,000. This would have to be compared with real estate values in the area, and with potential sales and profits.

C) Herbert would have a number of questions to ask such as: Why is the store empty? Is the space good for a variety store? How is the landlord? Is the location convenient to where he will be living?

Choice 2: The Small Variety Store

A) The store appears to be reasonably priced: $100,000 in total plus the rent of $18,000 per annum.

B) The lease is for two years plus an option for five more, so Herb could leave after two years if he is not happy with the business and/or the city.

C) Herbert has bought a store in the past and been successful. This experience is a plus.

D) Herbert would also have numerous questions to ask in this situation. These include: Why is the store for sale? What is it actually worth? Are there hidden reasons for the sale? How long have these people been in business? How do the financial statements appear? What are the supplier relationships like? What competition is there? What is the landlord like?

Choice 3: The Franchise

A) Payback is suggested within five years, which means $70,000 a year.

B) Herbert's temperament might be such that he will not be able to co-operate with the franchisor.

C) This is a major franchise; therefore, it is probably very successful and will have an established name that Herb can use.

D) Herbert would have to know a tremendous amount more about the franchise. Some questions would include: What sort of market research has been done, especially since this is one of the last city franchises, and therefore, potentially one of the worst? What sort of training is given? What royalties must be paid? How happy are existing dealers? What supplies must be purchased from the parent organization? What is the possibility for future expansion?

Alternatives

A) Choose one of the three options presented.

B) Keep searching for other potential sites.

C) Stay in Bleekersville.

Recommendations

Herbert appears ready to leave Bleekersville to test life in the city and expand options for his children. He has made initial inquiries to a real estate agent who has provided him with three options, but the information provided thus far is sketchy. Herbert must check into each of these options: answering the questions analyzed in the choice analysis and many others before making a decision. Based on the limited information given though, the franchise option seems least realistic based on Herbert's temperament. The small operating variety store is the most feasible choice, based on Herbert's experience in the past, and the fact that he can leave after two years if he is unhappy with the operation or city life. Herbert must avoid being too anxious to buy, settling for a second-rate operation, and should check with other realtors and on his own for potential business sites.

CASE FOUR: BARB'S BLUES

Problem

Barb cannot decide what computer is best for her business.

Sub-problems

1) Barb appears to need help in understanding computers.

2) Barb has a limited amount of funds with which to buy a computer.

Analysis

Barb's rapidly growing business is forcing her to expand control systems. Currently, she hires an accountant at tax time, but she cannot afford this service on a monthly basis, nor can she afford the time to maintain the general ledger herself. Barb is searching for the best cost-benefit solution to her problem.

Alternatives

1) This option is moderately expensive. Barb must dearly establish what this computer can do for her. What are the software capabilities? Given that the salesman has not been very helpful, will the dealer be able to answer questions later when almost inevitable snags occur?

2) This dealer is dearly interested in selling equipment rather than service. The price of the hardware is very attractive. Clearly this option only solves part of the problem.

3) This option offers what Barb actually wants. A major outstanding question is long-term support. If this guy is so busy, it is doubtful that he will have the time or inclination to provide high quality service. Considering the size of her business, the cost of this system is probably not worthwhile.

4) A consultant can provide Barb with expert knowledge. If this advice can reduce outlays for equipment and training, the cost of the consultant might be recovered. The consultant can provide Barb with a measure of security. It is important for Barb to check out this consultant's credentials, talk to former clients, etc.

5) Her most viable alternative to buying a computer is hiring a bookkeeper part-time. Estimating about 10 hours per week at $15 an hour, the bookkeeper would cost about $7,500 annually.

Recommendations:

First Barb has to come up with a cost-benefit estimate of a computer solution. Currently, Barb is having difficulty controlling her rapidly growing business; therefore, a new system must be set in place. Though a bookkeeper would be a potential option, a computer would be less expensive in the long term. If a computer can cut the time required to complete these tasks in half, and she can train one of her own employees to operate it, the cost could be reduced to about $3000 per year. Partially offsetting these savings is a demand on her own time during the implementation process, but this will not seriously reduce the benefit of this solution.

By looking at these four options, Barb has gained a lot of knowledge about buying a computer. Option #3, the "turnkey" system, though prohibitively expensive, has shown her actual examples of the applications she needs. This has helped her to define her ultimate goal. The two computer dealers have given her a good idea of the tremendous spread in computer prices.

None of these options seem ideal for Barbara. Given that her desires are really fairly standard for a small business, she should be able to find what is needed at one of the chain stores. Given the poor service at the first store, it would probably be worth her while to scout out another store or two, and purchase from a reputable outfit with a diligent staff.

This alternative seems viable. Using the consultant should help reduce Barb's time during the implementation. She will have to be careful and make sure that a good maintenance contract is negotiated with the hardware dealer.

CASE 5: JOAN'S STUFFED DOLLS

Problem
1. Should Joan start her own business? Can she afford to?
2. If Joan does start the business, should she commence operations from home or open a store?

Sub-Problems
1. Is there a market for Joan's dolls if they are priced far higher than the current $10? What market should Joan sell to?
2. Will Joan find that she becomes bored by her hobby turned business?
3. If Joan starts the empire, should she do it on a part or full-time basis?

Analysis
1. Don and Joan need to have a second income. It is critical, therefore, that Joan continues to make some money.
2. There does seem to be a demand for Joan's dolls. She has sold over 70 dolls in the past. Currently, at stores around Toronto, there are numerous dolls similar to Joan's that appear to be selling well. The quality of Joan's dolls appear to be comparable to or better than dolls currently on the market.

3. Joan does have experience making her dolls, but she has never had to make them in quantity. If she does start to produce in quantity, she may become bored with this work.

4. No information is given in the case as to the size of Don and Joan's home. Certainly it is big enough so that she can make one doll at a time, and it is probable that there would be enough space to store materials in some quantity.

5. It appears that Joan has the option to work as a legal secretary part-time. This would allow her to make dolls part-time and guarantee an income.

6. Numerical analysis: Joan will certainly want to know how much she can make from the business. The projections are based on the assumption that Joan sells all of her production m not necessarily the case.

Option A

Joan works full-time (250 days a year), and sells to retailers and friends for $55, half of the Yorkville cost.

Step 1

Calculate the profit per doll:

$$\text{Profit per doll} = \$55.00 - \$10.00 \text{ (cost)}$$
$$= \$45.00$$

Step 2

Calculate the income per year and per hour of labour. Based on 250 dolls per year (1 doll per day)

$$\text{Profit per doll} \times \text{Working days}$$
$$= \$45.00 \times 250$$
$$= \$11,250 \text{ annual income}$$

Based on 2000 hours of labour: $11,250 – 2000 (250 days x 8 hours) = $5.62 per hour of labour

Option B

Joan does both jobs part-time.

In this scenario Joan would earn $5,625 from the doll making, (half of her full-time income in Option A) plus half of her salary from the law firm.

Option C

Joan works full-time doll making and sells the dolls at $95, slightly less than the Yorkville rate.

Step 1

Calculate the profit per doll
$$\text{Profit per doll} = \$95.00 - \$10.00$$
$$= \$85.00$$

Step 2

Calculate the income per year and per hour of labour.
$$\text{Profit per doll x Working days}$$
$$= \$85.00 \times 250$$
$$= \$21,250 \text{ annual income or } \$10.62 \text{ per hour.}$$

Option D

Joan works as legal secretary part-time and makes dolls part-time. In this case she will make half of the annual income in Option C which is $10,625 plus her salary from the law firm.

Option E

Joan works full-time making dolls and sells half of her production at $95 and half at $55.
Under this option Joan will make:

$$\frac{(11,250 + \$21,250)*}{2}$$
$$= \$16,250 \text{ or } \$8.13 \text{ per hour}$$

Option F

Joan works at both jobs part-time and sells half her production at $95 and half at $55. In this case, she will make half of the doll making income or $8,125 plus her legal secretary wage.

Option G

Joan forgets the idea and continues to work full-time as a legal secretary. This would maintain her current income, but probably not make her very happy.

---

*Joan's annual salary under the two income plans. (Divided by 2 because two years are used in the calculations).

Alternatives

1. Joan can continue to work as a legal secretary full-time and make dolls a couple of times a month. Unfortunately, she seems bored by this option and a change seems to be desirable.

2. Joan can start making dolls full-time. If she sells all of her dolls at $95, her salary would be comparable to that of a legal secretary. But there is a major risk here. As her salary is necessary for the mortgage, making dolls full-time greatly increases the risk factor if the sales do not pan out.

3. Joan can work part-time as a legal secretary and part-time as a doll maker. This possibility might solve most of her difficulties. It can ensure a continuous flow of income from her legal secretary job and also allow Joan to utilize other skills that she enjoys. Also this might help her to reduce the boredom factor of doing any job full-time.

4. If Joan opens the business, she might open a store. This option, though, does not seem feasible as the expenses associated with opening a store would be prohibitive for Joan to assume. Also, she has no experience in this field and would almost certainly fail.

5. Joan can work from the house. This seems to be the most likely situation. It would keep her costs down dramatically and save her time travelling from the house to the store.

Recommendations

Joan should try the business on a part-time basis. This would seem to satisfy most of her needs. It would guarantee Don and herself one and a half incomes even if the business produces no results. By starting part-time, Joan would also be able to build up clientele more slowly. It would be best for Joan to sell the dolls herself first, to family and friends, or through trade fairs and flea markets, as this will lead to the highest profits, before approaching retail outlets. Joan should commence the business from the home, as the start-up costs of a store and her lack of experience make this option foolhardy.

In the longer term, if Joan finds that the business is a success and wishes to pursue it full-time, she will already have made inroads into the marketplace. She will also have a better idea if she will enjoy doing this work full-time, so the "boredom quotient" would have been tested. Also, production time will probably be reduced substantially, as Joan will likely adopt an "assembly line" approach to doll making.

If Joan finds that the business is a big success, at some point in the future she might wish to hire employees or begin a retail store. If this is a potential aim, she should consider compatible products that she might wish to sell in the store.

Last, if the business is a dismal failure, as sales do not appear or Joan finds her desire to make dolls wanes, she will have retained her position as a legal secretary part-time. It will, therefore, be easier to return to this work full-time than if she had left the job.

Ultimately, by starting the business part-time from the home, keeping her job part-time, and testing the marketplace further, Joan will greatly reduce her risk. This is a key element when considering starting a new business.

CASE 6: THE JONSON SAGA: PART I

Problem

The Jonsons* want to answer some basic marketing questions: Who will their customers be? When will their busy season be? Where will they cater? Why will people buy their products? How should they promote the business?

Sub-Problem

Formulating part of their marketing plan with this information.

Analysis
Who will their customers be?

The Jonsons will be dealing with two target markets. Within the first group, the majority of the customers will be middle-and upper-class women, between the ages of 30 and 65. In many cases, a man will provide the funding for the catering, but a woman will make the catering choice. The woman, therefore, is the target market. In the second group will be businesses, sporting groups, associations, clubs, hotels, and convention centres. In most cases, the buyer will be designated by the organization holding or hosting the function.

---

*Dave really wants to know this too. He just could not tear himself away from "Dallas."

Where will they cater?

The catering will be delivered to people's homes, banquet halls, sporting clubs, hotels, etc.

When will the busy season be?

The Jonsons will have two primary busy seasons. The first will be from May to July, the prime wedding season. The second major season will be the Christmas and New Year period, which for the Jonsons would last from mid-November to the beginning of January. Because the business has seasonal cycles, the Jonsons will have to plan to have sufficient cash-on-hand to purchase inventory, perhaps hire another employee, and to make certain that their distribution needs are being met during the busy periods.

Why will people buy their products?

People will buy from the Jonsons primarily because of the quality of their goods. This will be a key success variable.

Service will also be extremely important. Price will be a consideration, but a lesser priority for most of the clientele.

How should the Jonsons promote the business?

The Jonsons will have limited resources to promote the business; therefore, they will have to consider promotional methods that will give them the "best bang for their small buck" and allow them to serve their two prime target markets: wealthy women who give parties; and businesses, clubs, hotels, etc.

Flyers delivered in affluent areas would be a relatively inexpensive and efficient method of advertising to the wealthy clientele, but the Jonsons must make certain that the flyers conform with their business image. Personal selling would probably be best when dealing with hotels, clubs, and associations. The Jonsons should meet with the purchasing representative of the organization and perhaps entice the buyer with some samples of their preparations.

Another technique that the Jonsons should utilize is free promotion. The Jonsons would be wise to contact their local newspapers, radio and television stations, and see if perhaps they could use a good story about a new local business. Perhaps the Jonsons can have a local radio station offer a fully catered meal as a prize for a contest; or perhaps Dolly can prepare food on a local television station. By being innovative, the Jonsons can obtain all kinds of free publicity.

Other options such as paid television advertisements, radio, magazine, and newspaper spots are worth considering, but are probably beyond the means of the Jonsons budget. If they did choose to use one of these media types, then they would be wise to select the medium that related directly to their target market. A bridal magazine, or a glossy lifestyle magazine, would make a good selection.

Alternatives

In this case, there are few alternatives. The Jonsons must select an appropriate media type that is consistent with their image, clientele, and budget. Also, they must consider exactly how to approach their customers. These choices were discussed in the analysis.

Recommendations

The Jonsons are thinking of starting a business where quality is the key success variable. For this reason, it is important that they do not take on more work than they can handle efficiently, otherwise they might develop a poor reputation. They must also make certain that they plan for their seasonal fluctuations. By honing in on their target markets, the Jonsons should realize that they have two market segments to serve. With this information, the Jonsons should develop an overall marketing plan to reach both target audiences, with specialized marketing to reach the middle- and upper-class sector, and a direct sales plan to serve businesses, hotels, sporting clubs, etc. This technique is fairly common where different marketing plans are adopted for the business's various target markets.

CASE 7: JIM'S FIX-IT: PART 1

Problem

Jim Jones had to prepare a balance sheet and income statement.

Sub-Problem

The only one may be that Jim Jones's accountant might need to lose weight.

Analysis

See Income Statement and Balance Sheet.

Jim's Fix-It
Income Statement: Year Ending January 15, XXXX

Net Sale		$42,000
Cost of Goods Sold		21,000
Gross Profit		21,000
Expenses		
Salaries	$3,000	
Hydro	3,000	
Telephone	400	
Building Depreciation	7,500	
Equipment Depreciation	1,200	
Miscellaneous	900	
Total Expenses		16,000
Net Profit Before Tax		5,000
Income Tax		1,250
Net Profit After Tax		$3,750

Jim's Fix-It — Balance Sheet — January 15, XXXX

ASSETS
Current Assets

Cash	$12,000
Accounts Receivable	4,000
Inventory	3,600
Total Current Assets	19,600

Fixed Assets

Building	$75,000	
Less: Accumulated Depreciation	22,500	52,500
Office Equipment	1,500	
Less: Accumulated Depreciation	1,200	300
Goodwill		1,000
Total Fixed Assets		53,800
Total Assets		$73,400

LIABILITIES
Current Liabilities

Accounts Payable	$ 6,000
Notes Payable	10,000
Hydro Payable	400
Taxes Payable	1,500
Total Current Liabilities	17,900
Long-Term Liabilities	
Note Payable	30,000
Total Long-Term Liabilities	30,000
Total Liabilities	47,900

NET WORTH

Retained Earnings	25,500
Total Net Worth	25,500
Total Liabilities & Net Worth	$73,400

Alternatives
There are no alternatives presentable from this case. Income statements and balance sheets are specific as to their creation.

There are variations in accounting procedures, but none that would have an impact upon this case.

Recommendations
Jim Jones can prepare his own income statement and balance sheet. This will increase Jim's understanding of his venture and aid him in making strategic decisions for the benefit of his enterprise. This does not diminish the value of an accountant.

The accountant in this case should join the YMCA.

CASE 8: JIM'S FIX-IT: PART 2

Problem
Doing all of the assorted entries and then completing a new income statement and balance sheet.

Sub-Problem
How will Mr. Chubby buy the Tom Forrestall painting if more clients become independent?

Analysis
Step 1
List the transactions

	Accounts	Debit	Credit
1) January 22	Cash	3000	
	Sales		3000
2) January 22	Car	2000	
	Cash		2000
3) January 22	Cash	200	
	Acc. Rec.	200	
	Sales		400
4) January 23	Wage Exp.	400	
	Cash		400
5) January 23	Note Pay.	1000	
	Cash		1000
6) January 24	Depr. Exp.	300	
	Acc. Depr. Equip.		300
7) January 25	Cash	500	
	Sales		500
8) January 26	Cash	300	
	Acc. Rec.		300

Step 2
Post to T accounts

Cash	
12000	
3000	1
2	2000
200	3
4	400
5	1000
500	7
300	8
12600	

Acc. Rec.	
4000	
200	3
8	300
3900	

Inventory	
3600	
3600	

Building	
75000	
75000	

Building Depr.	
	22500
	22500

Office Equip.	
1500	
1500	

Equipment Depr.	
	1200
6	300
	1500

Goodwill	
1000	
1000	

Accounts Payable	
	6000
	6000

Notes Payable	
	40000
1000	5
	39000

Hydro Payable	
	400
	400

Taxes Payable	
	1500
	1500

Retained Earnings	
	25500
	25500

Sales	
1	3000
3	400
7	500
	3900

Car	
2000	2
2000	

Wage Expense	
400	4
400	

Depr. Exp.	
300	6
300	

Step 3
Adjusting Entries

12) January 26   C.G.S.   950
                    Inventory   950

Cost of Goods Sold		Inventory	
950	9	9	950
950			950

Step 4
Closing Entries
13) Jan. 26   Income Summary   1650
                    Wage Expense   400
                    Equip. Depr. Exp.   300
                    C.G.S.   950

14) Jan. 26   Sales   3900
                    Income Summary   3900

Sales		Income Summary		Wage Expense	
3900	14	1650	13	13	400
3900		14	3900		400
			2250		

Equip. Depr. Exp.		C.G.S.		Net Income	
13	300	13	950	2250	15
	300		950	2250	

Retained Earnings	
15	2250
	2250

Step 5 (see page 262)

Step 6
Prepare an Income Statement and a Balance Sheet.

Step 5

The Trial Balance

Account	Trial Balance Beginning	Transactions Debit	Transactions Credit	Adjustments Debit	Adjustments Credit	Closing Debit	Closing Credit	Income	Balance
Cash	12000	12600							12600
Acc. Rec.	4000	3900							3900
Inventory	3600	3600			950				2650
Building	75000	75000							75000
Building Deprecia.	22500	22500						22500	
Office Equipment	1500	1500							1500
Equipment Deprecia.	1200		1500				300		1500
Goodwill	1000	1000							1000
Acc. Pay.	6000		6000						6000
Notes Pay.	40000		39000						39000
Hydro Pay.	400		400						400
Taxes Pay.	1500		1500						1500
Ret. Earn.	25500		25500				2250		27750
Sales			3900			3900		3900	
Car		2000							2000
Wage Exp.		400					400	400	
Cost of Goods Sold				950			950	950	
Income Summary							2250		
Depr. Exp.		300						300	
Net Income					2250		2250		
	97100 = 97100	100300 = 100300		950 = 950		6150 = 6150	6150 = 6150		

Income Statement: Week Ending January 26, XXXX

Net Sales		$ 3,900
Cost of Goods Sold		950
Gross Profit		2,950
Operating Expenses		
Wage Expense	$400	
Depreciation Expense	300	
Total Expenses		700
Net Income Before Tax		$ 2,250

Jim's Fix-It Balance Sheet January 26, XXXX

ASSETS
Current Assets

Cash		$12,600
Accounts Receivable		3,900
Inventory		2,650
Total Current Assets		19,150

Fixed Assets

Building	$75,000	
Less: Accumulated Depreciation	22,500	52,500
Office Equipment	1,500	
Less: Accumulated Depreciation	1,500	000
Car		2,000
Goodwill		1,000
Total Fixed Assets		55,500
Total Assets		$74,650

LIABILITIES
Current Liabilities

Accounts Payable		$ 6,000
Notes Payable		9,000
Hydro Payable		400
Taxes Payable		1,500
Total Current Liabilities		16,900

Long-Term Liabilities

Note Payable	30,000
Total Long-Term Liabilities	30,000
Total Liabilities	46,900

NET WORTH

Retained Earnings	27,750
Total Net Worth	27,750
Total Liabilities & Net Worth	$74,650

Alternatives

The only real alternative in this case is to use a different bookkeeping system. Numerous other systems do exist.

Recommendations

Jim can do the bookkeeping himself, although this would not be wise before he has taken a course in this area. There are numerous inexpensive courses that can be studied.

Mr. Chubby should consider putting pictures on the wall done by his children, ages six and four. This would be far less expensive than purchasing a Tom Forrestall.

CASE 9: THE JONSON SAGA: PART 2

Problem

Dave and Dolly Jonson want to know their cash flow, and from this they will be able to decide if this aspect of their business appears feasible.

Sub-Problems

Dave and Dolly Jonson do not seem to like negotiating.

Analysis

First, the cash flow chart must be completed. (See page 265)

Budgeted Jonson Cash Flow Worksheet							
Month	Dec.	Jan.	Feb.	March	April	May	June
Cash on Hand	$2000	1200	1350	(550)	(900)	550	2000
Cash in: Sales	450	450	450	1350	1350	1350	1350
A/R	—	450	450	450	1350	1350	1350
Other	—	—	—	—	—	—	—
Total Cash In	450	900	900	1800	2700	2700	2700
Total Cash	2450	2100	2250	1250	1800	3250	4700
Cash Out: Rent	150	150	150	150	150	150	150
C.G.S.	300	300	300	900	900	900	900
Wages	100	100	100	100	100	100	100
Promotions	100	200	200	100	100	100	100
Renovations			900	900			
Incorporation	500						
Utensils	100		400				
Microwave			750				
Other	—	—	—	—	—	—	—
Capital expenditures: Have decided to calculate after one year.							
Replacements: Have decided to calculate after one year.							
Total Cash Out	1250	750	2800	2150	1250	1250	1250
Cash Flow from Operations	(800)*	150	(1900)	(350)	1450	1450	1450
Monthly Balance	$1200	1350	(550)	(900)	550	2000	3450

*Brackets indicate negative numbers.

Once the cash flow projection is completed, it can be seen that the Jonsons will have a cash flow shortage in February and March. The crunch hits when Total Cash Out jumps from $750 to $2800, causing a negative cash flow situation of $1900. In March, the negative cash flow situation persists, leaving a deficit of $900. Negative cash flow is not necessarily harmful, and is to be expected for the first year or two in most new businesses. But when a negative monthly balance is the result of the cash flow, then the danger of bankruptcy exists. To avoid this event, the Jonsons must decide on a method to alter their cash flow position.

Alternatives

1A) The Jonsons have chosen to pay for their microwave in one lump sum. Perhaps they can negotiate a payment plan. One suggested method of payment would be $250 down, with another $250 in each of April and May. This will help them to reduce their cash flow deficit by $500 in the key months of February and March and would remain a fair payment plan for most retailers. This method of "stretching accounts payable" is common and benefits the business tremendously.

1B) Another possibility is not to buy the microwave. This would severely curtail sales though, as sales increase in the month that the microwave is purchased.

2A) If the payments for the renovations were pushed back one month, then the Jonsons would never be in a negative cash position at the end of a month. If everything went according to plan, the lowest monthly balance would be reached in March when no money would be on hand, but no money would be owing. This solution could prove to be ideal.

2B) If the contractor would not agree to these terms, then the Jonsons should still attempt to negotiate a longer payment schedule — perhaps over a four month period of time. Another possibility is to delay the renovations for a month or two, although this would have a negative impact on sales for this period of time, as not as much food would be prepared.

3A) The payment plan could be changed to receive 50 percent of the money when the order was received, with the rest of the funds upon delivery of the merchandise. This would speed up the receivable collection; thereby improving the cash flow.

3B) Offering discounts to customers for quick payment might immediately improve the cash flow situation; Perhaps a one percent discount for full payments within ten days.

4) Perhaps the Jonsons can operate the business from the home. Insufficient evidence exists in the case concerning this option, but it should be considered.

5) The need for the employee should be evaluated. Maybe the Jonsons can do all of the work themselves, at least until the sales growth in February.

6) A bank might be approached for short-term financing. If this cash flow analysis was prepared with accompanying financial statements, the banker would probably recommend a loan, as he would see that the business is viable.

Recommendations

Dave and Dolly Jonson have a viable opportunity that will start to return them $1,450 a month once April is reached. The question is whether or not they can survive until April. By renegotiating the payment terms on the microwave and renovations, their difficulties should be resolved completely. In addition to this, they should alter their credit terms, demanding at least 50 percent of the cash when the order is received, and the rest of the payment upon delivery of the goods. A discount should also be carefully considered. If cash flow problems persist, then a banker should be approached for a short-term loan.

In the future, Dave and Dolly should negotiate payment and receivable terms carefully. This can improve their cash flow position and their profit level.

This case represents a typical business situation, where a potentially viable venture might not survive because the owners may not have formulated a cash flow projection. It is possible that creditors could place the Jonsons in bankruptcy, or they would simply become discouraged and disband the operation when their initial investment was spent, not realizing that success was just a couple of months away. By doing the cash flow projection, success or failure becomes recognizable.

CASE 10: A CASE ON WOOD AND STUFF

Problem
To find various break-even points which will help to indicate if the business is viable.

Sub-Problems
1. Is there a market for the business?
2. Will the partnership work?

Analysis
Part A
The number of cords necessary to break-even.

Step 1
Calculate the variable costs.

Wood	$45.00
Bags	5.00
Total	$50.00 of variable costs.

Step 2
Find the contribution.

Contribution = Selling Price – Variable Costs
= $100.00– $50.00
= $50.00

Step 3
Calculate the fixed costs.

Gas	$ 30.00
Labour	600.00
Promotion	300.00
Blades	20.00
	$950.00

Gas would vary slightly, as would the blades, but neither would vary significantly; therefore, they are considered to be fixed.

Step 4

Break-Even in Units = $\dfrac{\text{Fixed Costs}}{\text{Contribution Per Unit}}$

$\qquad = \dfrac{\$950}{\$50}$

$\qquad = 19 \text{ cords}$

Therefore 19 cords (units must be sold to break-even.)

Part B

With salaries, the number of cords that must be sold to break-even.

Step 1

Salaries become a fixed cost; therefore the total fixed costs are:

$$\text{Total Fixed Costs} = \$950 + 2000$$
$$= \$2950$$

Step 2

Break-Even in Units = $\dfrac{\text{Fixed Costs}}{\text{Contribution Per Unit}}$

$\qquad = \dfrac{\$2950}{\$50}$

$\qquad = 59 \text{ cords to break-even.}$

From Parts A and B the question that must be answered is: Can they realistically sell this many cords to make the operation viable?

Part C

The sales level necessary to break-even with salaries.

Break-Even in Sales \$ = Selling Price x Number of Cords

$\qquad = \$100.00 \text{ x } 59$

$\qquad = \$5,900 \text{ of revenues to break-even.}$

Alternatives

1) Go into the business.
2) Do not go into the business.

The decision on whether or not to enter the business will depend largely on Bill and Clarence's estimate of sales. Certainly the salaries that both men wish to make from the enterprise are not unreasonable, nor is the sales level needed to achieve this wage very high.

A personal assessment of the two individuals involved would be worthwhile, especially since Clarence is prone to failure. Do both of these gentlemen have the drive and ambition to make this business succeed? This is certainly a factor that will be important for success, and with Clarence's record, a huge question.

Recommendations

Financially, the business seems to have the potential for success. Both the sales and unit figures necessary to break-even are not high. But Clarence does not seem to have the skills necessary to be a prosperous businessperson. Four bankruptcies indicate a potential partner that Bill should avoid.

CASE 11: JILL'S CRAFTS

Problem

The major problem in this case is survival. Jill's business is in danger of going bankrupt.

Sub-Problems

1. Jill has lost control of her accounts receivable, inventory, debt, and accounts payable.
2. Jill's expenses have increased dramatically, particularly rent and wages.

Analysis

Profitability Ratios
1. R.O.I.

$$2000$$
$$5850 \div \frac{(5000 + 5000)}{2}$$
$$= 117\%$$

$$2001$$
$$6400 \div \frac{(5000 + 5000)}{2}$$
$$= 129\%$$

2002

$8800 \div \dfrac{(5000 + 5000)}{2}$

$= 176\%$

This is a tremendous return on investment that is improving annually. This should be compared with the interest rate at the bank, or other potential investments.

2. Gross Profit to Sales

2000	2001	2002
$\dfrac{6000}{8000}$	$\dfrac{9200}{12000}$	$\dfrac{15000}{19000}$
= 75%	= 76%	= 79%

This is a fairly minor variation which demonstrates that the Cost of Goods Sold is staying constant as a percentage of sales.

The debt has increased dramatically to the point where creditors have a larger stake in the business than the equity position. This is a real danger.

3. Net Profit to Sales

2000	2001	2002
$\dfrac{5850}{8000}$	$\dfrac{6450}{12000}$	$\dfrac{8800}{19000}$
= 73%	= 54%	= 46%

This ratio has taken a definite turn for the worse. This shows that expenses have increase dramatically as a percentage of sales.

Liquidity Ratios
1. Working Capital

2000	2001	2002
5000 – 1000	12000 – 45002	1000 – 10000
= $4,000	= $7,500	= $11,000

This is a positive trend as the working capital level is increasing.

2. Current Ratio

2000	2001	2002
5000:1000	12000:4500	21000:10000
= 5:1	= 2.7:1	= 2.1:1

The current ratio has moved to a point approximating a healthy indus-try average, but to do this it has dropped precipitously. At a 5:1 rate, assets are often not deployed as well as possible; therefore, the funds of the business might be being utilized poorly. But the steepness of this decline is questionable.

3. Acid Test

2000	2001	2002
$\frac{(5000 - 2000)}{1000}$	$\frac{(12000 - 5000)}{4500}$	$\frac{(21000 - 9000)}{10000}$
= 3:1	= 1.6:1	= 1.2:1

This is the same sort of situation as with the current ratio. The acid test appears healthier now than in 2000, but the drop has been so swift as to be potentially lethal.

4. Debt/Equity

2000	2001	2002
$\frac{0}{5000}$	$\frac{3300}{5000}$	$\frac{6600}{5000}$
= 0	=66%	=132%

The debt has increased dramatically to the point where creditors have a larger stake in the business that the equity position. This is a real danger.

5. Age of Accounts Receivable

2000	2001
$1000 \div (8000 \div 360)^{*}$	$3000 \div (12000 \div 360)$
= 45 days	= 90 days

2002

$11000 \div (19000 \div 360)$

= 208 days

*These calculations can also be done with 365 days instead of 360 days. The results will not dif-fer appreciably.

Jill has lost control of her accounts receivable. Perhaps she is too nice to demand her money.

6. Age of Inventory

2000	2001	2002
$2000 \div \dfrac{(2000)}{360}$	$3000 \div \dfrac{(2800)}{360}$	$9000 \div \dfrac{(4000)}{360}$
= 360 days	= 643 days	= 810 days

Jill has completely lost control of her inventory. This can lead to obsolescence, damage, and generally increased costs.

7. Age of Accounts Payable[**]

2000	2001	2002
$1000 - \dfrac{(2000)}{360}$	$3000 - \dfrac{(2800)}{360}$	$8000 - \dfrac{(4000)}{360}$
= 186 days	= 386 days	= 720 days

The age of accounts payable has also increased dramatically, but even if Jill wanted to, she does not have the funds available to pay them.

Growth Ratios
1. Sales Growth

2000-2001	2001-2002
$\dfrac{(1200 - 8000)}{8000}$	$\dfrac{(19000 - 12000)}{12000}$
= 50%	= 58.3%

Sales have been growing wonderfully. There is obviously a demand for this business.

2. Profit Growth

2000-2001	2001-2002
$\dfrac{(6450 - 5850)}{5850}$	$\dfrac{(8800 - 6450)}{6450}$
= 10.2%	= 36.4%

Though profit has been increasing, it has not undergone the same rapid

---

[**] Because purchases are not known, cost of goods sold should be used.

growth as sales. This indicates difficulties in the operation.

3. Asset Growth

2000-2001	2001-2002
$\dfrac{(12800 - 6000)}{6000}$	$\dfrac{(21600 - 12800)}{12800}$
= 113%	= 68.8%

This gives a more glowing report than is actually the case, as when the numbers are examined in relation to the other ratios, the increase is recognized as being primarily accounts receivable and too much inventory.

4. Debt Growth

2000-2001	2001-2002
$\dfrac{(7800 - 1000)}{1000}$	$\dfrac{(16600 - 7800)}{7800}$
= 680%	= 113%

Even though debt growth has slowed appreciably, this is still an increasingly dangerous situation.

Jill's business presents a paradox. The revenues and profits are increasing substantially, but she is moving closer and closer to bankruptcy. The major reason for this is because Jill has lost control of her accounts receivable and inventory. The age of receivables has reached 208 days. This is the average age! The inventory takes over two years to turn over. This is horrendous. Because of these major difficulties, Jill has not been able to pay down her accounts payable and has been forced to assume additional debt, so much so that bankruptcy is imminent.

Alternatives

1. Jill must collect on her accounts receivable. She must start to "hound" customers for payment. Phone calls and personal visits must be deployed. For some accounts, she might even consider offering a discount if they pay within ten days. Though this is not normal business operating practice for overdue accounts, the incentive might induce some customers to pay. Better to receive some money than none at all! The accounts that Jill recognizes as being uncollectable should be listed as

expenses. By doing this, the taxable income will be reduced, so at least a limited benefit will be received.

2. Inventory is at an outrageous level. Jill's rent has increased dramatically, probably because of the space she needs for the inventory. By reducing inventory, Jill will likely receive the benefit of reduced rent, plus less damage, waste, and employee time spent in this area. A sale would be a viable option. This would allow Jill to obtain cash to reduce her debt, eliminate inventory — some of which is probably in sad condition — and improve her cash flow situation.

3. Wages have risen dramatically. Perhaps the employee is not necessary. This situation should be carefully evaluated.

4. Jill should contact suppliers and explain why she is so late paying them. This might help to improve relations.

Recommendations

Jill Friendly has a viable venture that is being grossly mismanaged. By chasing customers with outstanding accounts, and having a sale to reduce inventory, Jill should be able to obtain the necessary funds to reduce her debt load and pay off her suppliers. Once this is done, the need for space should be re-evaluated, as should the necessity of the employee.

For the long-term, Jill should establish a policy to collect her accounts receivable. She should also implement methods to control her inventory. By doing these things, Jill's Crafts has a chance to grow and prosper. But if these actions are not taken quickly, Jill might be soon be looking for a new line of work.

Appendix II
Glossary

A

ACCOUNT: a record of a business transaction

ACCOUNT RECEIVABLE: money owed to the business by customers

ACCOUNT PAYABLE: money owed to suppliers by the business

ACCOUNTANT: usually a trained professional who keeps books

ADVERTISING: a public announcement usually designed to persuade

ASSET: something of worth that is owned

B

BALANCE SHEET: the financial statement that shows what a business owns and owes

BONDED WAREHOUSE: a warehouse where goods are stored in bond

BOOK VALUE: the firm's worth on paper

BREAK-EVEN POINT: the point at which total costs equal total revenues, therefore no profit or loss is made

BUDGET: a monetary plan

BUSINESS CYCLE: the variations in the business economy as it expands and contracts, leading to prosperity, recession, and depression

BUSINESS PLAN: a written outline of the overall objectives and activities of the business enterprise

C

CAPITAL: money available for and/or within the business; also often refers to assets available for production

CAPITAL COST ALLOWANCE: depreciation for income tax purposes

CASH FLOW: money coming in and going out of the business

CASH DISCOUNT: a reduction for prompt payment

CHANNELS: the path the product follows from production until it reaches the consumer; every intermediary in the path is a channel

COMPLEMENTS: goods that are used together

CONTRACT: an agreement between two or more parties

COPYRIGHT: protects original or cultural works in the areas of publishing, producing, reproducing, or performing

CORPORATION: a business entity distinct in law from the individuals who own the business

COST-BENEFIT ANALYSIS: an area of analysis that weights the costs of a decision to the benefits received

COST OF GOODS MANUFACTURED: amount of goods sold by a manufacturing firm

COST OF GOODS SOLD: amount of goods sold by a non-manufacturing firm

CREDIT: 1) the right side of an account; "to credit" means to change the right side of the account; 2) money owing because of the belief in a person's willingness to pay

CRITICAL PATH: a timetable so that a major event will be completed on schedule

CURRENT ASSET: goods that the business expects to turn into cash within one year

CURRENT LIABILITY: the amount of money that the business owes and must pay within one year

D

DEBIT: the left side of an account; "to debit" means to change the left side of an account

DEBT: that which is owed

DEMAND: would-be purchasers for a good or service

DEPRECIATION: a decrease in value through age and deterioration

DISTRIBUTION: the act of moving the products to the marketplace

E

ECONOMIES OF SCALE: the larger the organization, the lower the cost per unit to reach the marketplace; at a certain size, diseconomies of scale can set in

ENTREPRENEUR: a person who operates a business

F

FIFO (first-in, first-out): an accounting method based on the principle that the first inventory received is the first inventory sold

FINANCIAL STATEMENTS: documents that show a financial situation

FIXED ASSETS: items that will last longer than one year that are to be used in the operation of the business but are not intended for resale

FIXED COSTS: costs that do not vary with sales but stay the same

FIXED SUM SITUATION: a relationship in which a gain for one party means a loss for another

FRANCHISE: an agreement that a buyer may sell the product or service that another party has title to

FRANCHISEE: someone who obtains a franchise

FRANCHISOR: the person or company who sells the franchise

G

GENERAL PARTNERSHIP: a partnership in which all of the partners share in the management of the business and have unlimited liability for any losses incurred

GROSS PROFIT: the profit figure after subtracting the cost of goods sold or manufactured from the sales

I

IMPULSE BUY: a spur-of-the-moment decision to purchase

INCOME: money coming in

INCOME STATEMENT: the financial statement showing profit or loss

INDUSTRIAL DESIGN: products made by a manufacturing process that have an original shape, pattern, or ornamentation

INVENTORY: ultimately, the assets a business has for sale

J

JOURNAL: a record of all accounting transactions that must be debited or credited within an accounting period

K

KEY SUCCESS VARIABLES: factors that are crucial to a business's success

L

LEASE: a rental agreement

LEDGER: a book to keep track of bookkeeping transactions

LIABILITY: something owed

LIABILITY INSURANCE: Protection for actions for which a business is liable

LIFO (last-in, first-out): an accounting method based on the principle that the last inventory received is the first inventory sold

LIMITED PARTNERSHIP: a partnership in which some of the partners have limited liability

LOAN: money that is lent

LUXURIES: desirable but not indispensable goods

M

MANUFACTURER IN BOND: an individual who received alcoholic goods and products

MANUFACTURING: the conversion of raw materials into a useful product

MARKET MODIFICATION: search for new market segments that might buy your product or a repositioning of the product so that increased usage might result

MARKET NICHE: a specialized portion of a market

MARKET PENETRATION STRATEGY: a strategy designed to make fast inroads into a market by offering a low price

MARKET SEGMENTATION: the process of dividing the population into segments

MARKET SHARE: the percentage of the marketplace that a business sells to

MARKETING: the activities involved in selling a product

MARKETING MIX: the "Four P's" of marketing: Place, Price, Product and Promotion

MIDDLE PERSON: the individual who transfers goods between man-ufacturers and retailers

N

NAME SEARCH: the process of making certain that a proposed name is not already in use

NECESSITIES: indispensable items

NET PROFIT: profit after all charges are deducted

NOTE PAYABLE: money that is usually owed to bankers

O

ORDER POINT: the time at which inventory should be ordered

P

PARTNERSHIP: a partnership exists when two or more persons combine their funds and abilities to carry on a business for profit

PATENT: protection for an invention or innovation

PEAK: the end of the expansion of a business cycle

PENT-UP DEMAND: product that exists and is waiting for a product or service to fill that need

POINT-OF-PURCHASE DISPLAYS: items strategically placed, usually near the cash register, to stimulate purchases

POSTING: to enter into an account

PRICE ELASTICITY: the change in quantity of a product consumed relative to the change in price

PRIME RATE: the lending rate banks give to their best customers

PRODUCT LIFE CYCLE: the process in which a product is introduced into a marketplace, experiences a growth in sales, before sales mature and begin to decline, possibly leading to the demise of the product

PRODUCT MODIFICATION: a product change to increase usage

PROMOTION: the area comprised of sales promotion, advertising, personal selling and publicity

PROPRIETORSHIP: a business owned by one person who is legally responsible for all of the business debts and other legal obligations

R

RATIO ANALYSIS: a method of analysing a business by looking at the balance sheet and income statement

RECESSION: an economic downturn characterized by rising unemployment levels, falling profit levels, and bankruptcies; when times are extremely difficult, this can become a depression

RETAIL: selling directly to the consumer

RETAINED EARNINGS: profits earned by the business that have been reinvested within the business

S

SERVICE: a business that sells personal skills rather than a product

SUBSTITUTE: goods that can be used in place of other goods

SUPPLY: goods available for consumption

T

T ACCOUNT: the changes in assets, liabilities and equities over time

TARGET MARKET: the group most likely to buy the product or service

TAX: contribution levied for support of government

TIME VALUE OF MONEY: the idea that a dollar today is worth more than a dollar tomorrow

TRADEMARK: a drawing, logo, phrase, shape or symbol used to distinguish the goods or services of one group from another

TROUGH: the end of the contraction phase of a business cycle

V

VARIABLE COSTS: costs that vary with sales

VENTURE CAPITALIST: investors who provide equity, usually for a stake in the business

W

WHOLESALER: the middle person between manufacturers and retailers; sometimes, but more rarely, the middle person between manufacturers and consumers

WORKING CAPITAL: money used in the daily operation of the business

Appendix III
The Goods and Services Tax
(GST)

The government implemented the Goods and Services Tax (GST) as of January 1, 1991, making the vast majority of goods and services taxable. At the same time as this new tax was implemented, the Federal Sales Tax of 13.5 percent was removed. This has made some items more expensive and others less expensive. For various reasons, none of which I will attempt to discuss here as that would mean reading the mind of government, this was deemed to be more effective. Therefore, most businesses will be in the position where they must both pay and collect this tax. Essentially, even though there has been tremendous controversy over its implementation, the GST is simply another of the many taxes that Canadians must deal with.

Who Pays

All persons, businesses and organizations with annual sales of over $30,000 in GST-taxable goods and services must register with the government. This is important for two reasons: a) it is against the law not to register; b) only by registering can you reclaim the money on your GST related purchases. Once enlisted, the government will send you a GST number.

Organizations which do not reach this $30,000 level retain the option of not registering. But it must be kept in mind that by not enrolling, GST related taxes on purchases, called "Input Tax Credits," cannot be recovered. These Input Tax Credits will make it worthwhile for the vast majority of enterprises to register their operation.

Another advantage of registering is so that your GST number shows on your invoices. This will aid your customers in claiming their own Input Tax Credits.

EXEMPT GOODS AND SERVICES

Some goods and services will be GST exempt. Organizations providing only these commodities will not have to register. Some of these items include: most dental and medical services; residential housing previously owned or for sale; legal aid; most financial institution services; farm products; fish and seafood for human consumption and groceries. Also, some activities by charities and non-profit organizations which are voluntary or non-profit, along with goods and services provided by public service enterprises remain non-taxable.

Other GST exempt items include: membership dues necessary to keep professional status by statute; exams or courses to maintain or obtain professional status; and cars that are leased exclusively for business purposes. Revenue Canada Excise Offices (see page 121/122) should be contacted if there is any doubt whether the good or service is indeed excluded.

INPUT TAX CREDIT

The "Input Tax Credit" refers to the credit a business receives for GST paid when making purchases relating to the taxable products or services sold to the consumer. Credit can also be claimed for the GST paid on other items directly related to the enterprise. This money should be claimed when filing the GST tax return.

The manner of doing this is quite easy. The amount paid should be totalled and subtracted from the amount of GST collected. If the result is a positive number, more collected than paid, this difference is owed to the government and should be remitted; a negative amount, more paid than collected, will entitle you to a refund.

REMITTANCE SCHEDULES

GST payments are to be made in conjunction with the government's payment schedule although there is some flexibility here. Businesses earning over $6 million must submit monthly; those earning from $500,000 to $6 million can file quarterly; all others have the option of filing annually. These payments, as explained earlier, will be the difference between the tax received and the inputs paid.

For GST purposes, there are two choices for the fiscal year. The first is in correspondence with the businesses current fiscal year, while the second matches the calendar.

ACCOUNTING METHODS

The government has attempted to develop two simplified accounting methods for the GST, the "Quick Method" and "Streamlined Accounting Method."

The Quick Method was designed so that it is not necessary to keep track of Input Tax Credits or the bulk of expenses. For those businesses making major capital expenditures, there is a special exemption so that they are not disadvantaged. The method is calculated by multiplying sales by a specified percentage which the government has predetermined for each business area. The Quick Method option is available to businesses with annual sales and revenues under $200,000 or grocery and convenience stores with sales under $500,000 with at least 25 per cent being basic groceries. Accounting, financial consultants and legal firms are not allowed to use this system.

In the Streamlined Method it is not necessary to separate taxable and zero-rated goods, therefore new cash registers will not be required. Zero-rated means that no tax is charged for the good or service sold but one can claim an associated Input Tax Credit.

The Streamlined Accounting Method is available to retail merchants selling both taxable goods and zero-rated basic groceries. Those enterprises earning under $6 million are eligible to use this system until 1993, but only those earning less than $2 million are eligible after this date.

Enterprises that will use any of these systems must file a notice with Revenue Canada, Customs and Excise.

The GST is not as complex as it has been made to appear. Application forms and additional information can be obtained by contacting a Canada Customs and Revenue Agency. Tel: 1-800-959-5525. www.ccra.gc.ca

APPENDIX IV
PARTNERSHIP AGREEMENTS

This appendix was added to the second edition because many people reading this book are doing so with the intent of forming a partnership. Partnerships, as stated previously, are delicate arrangements. A large percentage of them do not work, for a variety of reasons. To avoid disputes and costly legal actions, a partnership agreement set in place at the beginning of the venture, will go a long way to making a possible divorce more palatable.

PARTNERSHIP AGREEMENT CHECK LIST

The partnership agreement should take into account the following areas:

1 a) the current date and the date that the partnership will commence;
  b) the type of partnership: limited or general;
  c) the name of the business;
  d) a brief description of the nature of the enterprise;
  e) where the business will operate from if known;

2 a) a description of each partners' position and job;
  b) the amount or percentage of capital to be contributed by each partner;
  c) a salary schedule;
  d) the division of profits including when and how much;

3 a) information as to access to the partner's books;
  b) the type of accounting system that will be used and the fiscal year that will be chosen;
  c) who the auditor will be;
  d) who will have signing authority at the bank and for cheques (two people are usually desirable for larger amounts);

e) who will have signing authority for contracts;

f) the type of insurance that the enterprise will have;

4 a) the manner of valuing the business;

b) the rights of sale to other parties;

c) the rights of a partner to compete with the business; (this is of particular consequence when a partner leaves the business, for whatever reason);

d) the manner of introducing a new partner to the enterprise; usually full agreement by all parties is ideal here;

e) the manner of eliminating a partner;

f) the manner of settling disputes; often an auditor is best as legal recourse can be extremely expensive;

g) the actions that will be taken in case of the bankruptcy of the enterprise; the death of a partner; or the desire for dissolution.

APPENDIX IV
INDEX

AGMV Marquis

MEMBER OF SCABRINI MEDIA

Quebec, Canada
2002